MULTIPLY YOUR SUCCESS

THE BUSINESS OWNER'S WORKBOOK FOR WEALTH & OPPORTUNITY

245 PROVEN WAYS TO TAKE YOU TO THE NEXT LEVEL

Philip Grundell **Andrew R Miller**

ISBN: 1548062189

ISBN-13:978-1548062187

245 PROVEN WAYS TO TAKE YOU TO THE NEXT LEVEL

5 strategy areas for business owners:
From personal dreams to financial ambitions
X
7 common challenges in each:
Your roadblocks along the way
X
7 practical action points:
Strategies, techniques and tips to help you through

Contents

ACKNOWLEDGEMENTS

Phil and Andrew are indebted to the following people for making this book happen:

Mark Beaumont-Thomas, for pulling the thing together and getting it into some sort of shape that people can actually read.

Aimee Grundell, for creating the cover design with very little to go on, and then remaining patient whilst we messed around with it.

Christine Simms, for giving us a fresh pair of eyes.

Introduction

The number one thing that business owners need to do to get what they want: Ask for help

Congratulations! By buying this book you have taken a small, but very important, step in the right direction.

Every year, the Department for Business, Innovation and Skills conducts a survey of micro, small and medium-sized businesses to find out their plans and their problems.

The most recent report came has just come out and it backs up a trend that we have seen in previous reports. From these surveys, it is very clear to us what the number one issue is that holds business owners back:

They don't ask for support from the right places.

From the report, two key facts emerged.

Fact 1: 69% of businesses are looking to grow over the next few years

Not a major shock. Surely most business are looking to grow? But the point is that the majority of businesses are actively interested in doing better next year than this year. The thing is, growth requires change, and to change you need to do things differently. If you're looking to do things differently, it would make sense to do some research about what to do and how to do it. Wouldn't it?

This is why the second fact is so staggering:

Fact 2: Only 7% of business owners asked the right questions to the right people

In fact, 67% of business owners didn't ask around at all. They just sat in their own little bubble, hoping that the answer would miraculously appear.
They probably ended up working a lot more hours, at a much lower level of efficiency, and justified the small increase they saw as a job well done.

When you do look at those people who made the effort to ask, you realise how poorly served the business community is for genuine, valuable help. Most people ended up asking questions around strategy, sales and marketing or team development to their accountants, solicitors and banks. These people are good at what they do but I'm afraid it doesn't include hard-nosed, practical, real life "how to run a business" advice.

If any business wants to improve and do better, in any way, then they need to ask the right questions to the right people.

By buying this book you have taken the first step towards being able to do just that. Before we explain how, you're going to have to do a bit of reading and a bit of thinking.

First of all, let us break things down a bit. From our experience, there are 5 main areas where business owners need help. These are the areas that we coach our clients around and teach people about in our workshops.

1. Personal strategy - Getting what you want on a personal level

There are several reasons why people have their own business rather than being employed but, ultimately, it's not all about the business. The underlying reasons will be personal. It might be security for your family or just about being in control. Whatever it is, the reasons are personal.

Unfortunately, it is very easy to get wrapped up in the workings of the business and then people either forget – or never clarify in the first place – exactly why they do what they do.

Knowing this and being mindful of it drives everything else.

2. Business strategy - Getting what you want from the business

Once your personal strategy has been established, your business strategy can then be developed to suit.

The trouble is, very few people have a clear business strategy in place. And I don't mean a business plan with 20 pages that will send people to sleep by page 3.
Most people muddle along and aim to do better than last year. But you need to know where you're going and how you're going to get there. Who you're going to be in the marketplace with and which clients you're looking to attract. When you know what your business strategy is, you can then work on the next three areas.

3. Sales strategy - Achieving more sales/revenue

We're not talking about sales techniques here, but breaking down the business strategy to work out where to focus your efforts and maximise your income.

- Ensuring that your products and your positioning are correct for the appropriate market.
- Having a proper system in place to make things work for you
- Understanding where you can raise prices and who you can sell more to.
- Having the right sales mindset.

4. Delivery strategy - Developing a better team and a better level of service

As sales increase, you're going to have to get better at delivering what's needed. And for that, you're going to need the right team around you.

- Understand the promise you have made your clients.
- Recruit and retain the right members of staff.
- Know and communicate the objectives to your team, so that they're all on board.
- Take control of your time and learn how to delegate properly.

5. Financial strategy - Having stronger financial control

If you try to grow without getting the cash right, then you're likely to end up in trouble. Lack of cash is the biggest constraint to growth – because growth requires cash.

All the previous elements need to be managed and juggled via the numbers, so you need a clear financial strategy to know when to hire, when to fire and when to borrow.

What now? Getting help.

Just about every problem or challenge faced by a business owner fits around these 5 categories. Growth, by its very nature, causes problems and challenges which need to be resolved QUICKLY.

What to do if you can't solve these straight away by yourself?

You ask for help!

Preferably, of course, from the right person. So, here's your opportunity. We're going to make it easy for you. We're going to give you the information that you need to either answer your own question, or work out the right question to ask.

Have a think about where your biggest issue is right now. The one stopping you from getting what you want. Into which of the five broad areas does it best fit?

Have a look through the content page and see which section best fits your situation. Then get reading and think how you can apply the learnings to your own business. There will be gaps. It's impossible to include everything. So, here's the deal.

If your specific question isn't answered, then you'll be able to ASK US about your specific issue and we'll MAKE SURE you get the answer.

Because if we don't know it, we'll know someone that will.

The only way to get what you want is to ask for it.

Who are Phil Grundell and Andrew Miller?

We are business advisors, mentors and coaches with a huge amount of experience in running and advising businesses. We are fed up with all the poor and vague advice that floats around, and believe that business owners deserve better. We guarantee results for our clients and dedicate ourselves to their success.

My name is Phil Grundell and I am an Impact Coach.

I believe that any business can be improved, any challenge solved and any opportunity brought to reality. This is through **focus** and **clarity**, which leads to **confidence** and then **belief** and **faith**.

I have spent 30 years in business and 44 years in change management, in the complex industry of textiles. My clients come to me because I'm a bruiser. I've been there, done it and I'm still going. They recognise that I know what I'm talking about and that I'm ready to help anyone.

Ultimately, my clients get great results, fast. There's no fluff and no BS, just straight talking action. The minimum I seek for my clients is a 3-times return on their investment - most get much more. **And I'll make sure you get results or you'll get your money back.**

In short, if I can't help you, you'll still be ahead.

For more information, visit The How Academy:
www.howacademy.co.uk

My name is Andrew Miller and I'm The Business Enjoyment Coach.

I believe that everyone should be able to enjoy work and life - at the same time - whilst getting the rewards that are important to them. To do that, business and life should not be looked at in isolation. One impacts on the other and vice versa.

My background as an insolvency practitioner meant that my job for 16 years was to run businesses, in very difficult and stressful circumstances. That has given me a unique insight into the pressures a director is under when running a business. The value of that insight is demonstrated by the fact that I was asked by the previous government to advise them on how to bring a level of personal support to companies in financial difficulty.

I am different from other coaches, in that it is rare to find someone with such fierce intelligence and hard-edged experience of business that is also able to demonstrate such levels of care and empathy. Amongst those who know me I am recognised as one of the most genuine, caring and supportive people around. Someone that you would want by your side.

I have, to date, published three books, all for owners at different stages of their business life cycle, but all focused on finding harmony between the business owners, their lives and their business.

Ultimately, my clients feel happier. They make more money with less stress, developing better habits that will last them a lifetime.

For more information, visit Business Enjoyment: www.businessenjoyment.com

How to use this book

This book is designed so that you can dip into it whenever you have an issue and find the information you need. We recommend you keep it close at hand so that you can easily grab it and refer to it as and when needed.

However, we also recognise that many people like to start at the beginning of things and work through. So, there is benefit in reading through the entire book from beginning to end, understanding what it contains – and then using it to dip into.

Please note, there is a lot of information here. If you are going to just skim through, you will not be able to absorb all the learnings in one go. In addition, many key concepts apply across numerous areas, so these points are repeated frequently.

For virtually every point, you will have to do some work of your own. You need to find a way that suits you to filter through everything to get to the areas you need to work on first.

At the end of each section there is a table that you can quickly fill in to establish your current situation. At the end of the book is a summary table which will allow you to carry through your results and give you a big picture overview. This will help you pin down which areas to focus on moving forwards.

When you know in which areas you need to focus, really take the time to benefit from the points raised. Sit with each individual point and let it sink in. Where does it apply to your business and how can you make it work for you? Really take the time to reflect on your thoughts and note down any conclusions or actions you need to take.

Your business and your actions are your responsibility. Consequently, there are no drawn out conclusions or summary at the end of this book. It ends when it ends.

However, we do invite you to contact us if there is any additional help that you need.

Developing your strategy

In the following sections, we're going to be giving you some ideas and prompts for developing strategies for the 5 key areas:

1. **Personal strategy**
2. **Business strategy**
3. **Sales strategy**
4. **Delivery strategy**
5. **Financial strategy**

Seven x7: In each section, we give you seven x7 points: seven areas to work on, each with 7 action points to look at. 7 is our sweet-spot number, giving you just the right number of action areas, not too few, not too many. Each of seven categories has 7 action areas, giving you Seven x7.

Don't be afraid to write notes directly onto these pages – This book is designed to be an active workbook, complete with action-point checklists at the end of each section. As you make progress, take pleasure in crossing through and ticking off items as you complete them.

Progress made in achieving the action points in this book will not only help you and your business, it is also a good, tangible, morale-boosting sign of action being taken.

A word or two around testing and measuring

An attendee at one of our workshops once asked me, "Is there anything in marketing that is always guaranteed to work?"

I told her that the only marketing activity that I know of which works every time is testing and measuring (T&M).

This is a phrase that will crop up a lot in this book, but what is T&M? It is about trying (investing in) new things to create improvements (testing) and then measuring the results to quantify and ensure that the improvements turn out as expected for your ROI.

T&M has been practised in sales and marketing since the earliest opportunities arose to do it, when most products were sold through advertising in newspapers and magazines.

Back then, marketers tested and measured the outcome from using different fonts, sizes of adverts, headlines, how the copy was written, colour or black and white, place in the newspaper or magazine etc. They tested everything to create an edge and to win out against their competitors.

Currently, marketers still do similar testing and measuring in the wider variety of marketing techniques that now exist. For example, in building a website, a good web builder will test the copy, the headlines, the visuals, colours, fonts, layout, etc. They will also check what visitors do, how long they stay on the website and where they spend their time. They will probably use a purpose-built system to do this such as Google Analytics. They will check the copy on the site to optimise it to make it easier for Search Engines to find (Search Engine Optimisation). And they will test and measure many other things to maximise outcomes from the website.

What is surprising is that, given that T&M always works in helping to optimise results from selling and marketing, relatively few business owners actually use it, even when it is really simple to apply and produces very high returns.
Let's illustrate T&M with an example. Vicky sends out an email to inform her customers about a new offer. She notes the open rate for the campaign is 3%. Now, she may be happy with that 3%, but there is nothing stopping her sending out the same email to all the customers who have not opened her first mail but making just one small change to the subject line. If she could do this once, twice or several times, then she may well increase her overall open rate by another 3% and thus double the effectiveness of her campaign. All this at very little extra cost.

This is testing and measuring in action. Now you may ask if it is applicable to all sales and marketing activities. My answer to this is that if you cannot test and measure your spending on any sales and marketing, then you must ask yourself whether you should be spending your money on it at all. Because if you do not apply testing and measuring, then how do you know your spending is yielding the best return?

This puts me in mind of a quote from the American businessman John Wanamaker:

"Half the money I spend on advertising is wasted; the trouble is, I don't know which half."

He should have tested and measured.

And so must you.

Part 1

Your personal strategy Seven x7

Seven common challenges in personal strategy

Your personal strategy Seven x7

Seven common challenges in personal strategy

Personal strategy challenge one:
I want to be happier. How can I enjoy life more?

A business is there to work for you, not the other way around. Consequently, everything you do should start with and be built around your personal agenda.

Here are 7 things to try out. Give all of them a go and choose the ones that work best for you.

1. **Work out what you want**

Set some personal goals.

What does 'happy' actually look like? Why do you do, what you do? What do you really want to do for people? How do you want to achieve that?

This section will focus on general tips but the follow up sections will give you some areas to focus on. How to enjoy your business; find more time in the day; and the different areas to look at, based around the concept of being RICH.

In other words, getting it right in Relationships, Income, Competence and Health, the four key areas that work together to bring balance and harmony into our lives.

2. Focus on the actions not the outcome

Be careful when setting goals. The goal should represent a direction you want to head in, not a 'make or break' must have. The more pressure you put on yourself to achieve a specific target, the less likely you are to benefit from it.

Enjoy the journey, not the destination.

3. Find the quick wins

Once you've set the direction you want to be heading for, in each area that's important to you, what small steps can you make that will have a BIG impact?

The 80/20 rule works everywhere, so look for the actions with the most leverage, and start there.

4. Slow down

If you've ever wondered what the phrase "More haste, less speed" means, it's this: Life is about quality, not quantity – and your brain is much more efficient when it isn't rushed.

Focus on doing fewer things, better. And find time to let the brain relax. Solutions will come quicker.

5. Set your intention

The overall goals give you a direction to head in but you need to find ways to keep reminding yourself what they are.

Before you go to bed at night, think about the day ahead and how you want it to go. And then, first thing in the morning, be clear about what you're going to be looking for and how you want to be that day. Tell your mind to start looking for opportunities and for the positive things in life.

You only find things that you're looking for.

6. Choose how to react

Life is whatever you make of it and so you have a choice in how you react to any situation. You can choose what and who comes into your life. You're 100% responsible for what happens and how you feel.

Every argument comes down to a miscommunication. Every bit of stress comes from an incorrect assumption. When things go wrong, don't start with blame. Ask, "How did I make this happen?"

7. Increase the positivity

If life is getting you down, always remember to look for the cause, not just the symptom. Then start with yourself and work outwards. Get rid of anyone or anything that drains your energy.

Train yourself to start looking at the positive in every situation. It does exist. Write down a list of things that you **do** appreciate about your life. Take the time to look back over what you've achieved to date. But ensure that you are always aware of how you are NOW.

Personal strategy challenge one:
I want to be happier. How can I enjoy life more?

Challenge checklist	**Doing this!**	**Do more!**	**Start doing!**
1: Work out what you want			
2: Focus on actions, not outcome			
3: Find the quick wins			
4: Slow down			
5: Set your intention			
6: Choose how to react			
7: Increase the positivity			
TOTAL			

Transfer your totals to the table on Page 308.

Personal strategy challenge two:
My business is a pain. How can I enjoy it again?

This is a contradictory phenomenon. The main reason that people work for themselves, rather than get a job, is so that they can do the things they want to do, when they want to do them, without someone else telling them what to do.

And THEN they find themselves working harder, getting stressed or not finding their results as rewarding as they might expect.

If you don't enjoy running your business, you might as well get a job.

Here are 7 things to try out. Give all of them a go and choose the ones that work best for you.

1. Set congruent goals

You need to work out what you want from your business. If things aren't as you'd like, then how do you want them to be?

Most business owners go wrong by not considering their personal goals. Your business should work for you, not the other way around, so make your business goals serve your personal goals.

2. Keep track

There are so many ways in which life can cause us stress and pressure and it's not always obvious why.

Your starting point is to note down situations when you get stressed. Then you can look at what it was about that situation that caused you to react in that way.

You won't get all the solutions, but you might work some out – and you will know the areas you need to explore.

3. Choose what you do

It's your business. Why do something you don't enjoy?

Yes, there needs to be a market for what you do, but start with you:

- Why did you start your business in the first place?
- What are the key things that you are passionate about?
- What things are you really good at?

Remember, everyone is unique – they have their own unique style. That means that there will be something that you are the best in the world at. Certainly, in your world.

Also, look at what you don't enjoy and what you're not good at. How can you remove these things from your task list? Eventually everything can be dropped, delegated or outsourced.

4. Check if success will make you happy

What is success? Only you can truly know that – and it may not be what other people would consider to be success. If the success you've had to date, or your projected definition of success, doesn't excite you or give you pleasure, then you need to re-define.

Many people feel the need to prove themselves to others. Even when the others are no longer there. If your drive to succeed is in order to "prove someone wrong", then this is coming from a negative place and whatever success that brings won't give you happiness.

So, go back to your personal goals and be clear. What do YOU really want?

5. Ensure you aren't trying to be someone you're not

There is a certain expectation on us to behave in a certain way. To be a strong, charismatic leader and to be perfect in all things. This is rarely who we actually are. The more we try to be someone that we're not, the more tiring and less enjoyable things become.

The more authentic you are, the more others will connect with you and the more likely you'll work with people you want to work with. Then you'll enjoy business more.
Balance is required. Don't dump all your issues on colleagues and clients. But show them that you're human, not a robot.

6. Talk to others

Running a business can be a lonely job and it can be very easy to lose touch with who you are. So, make sure you can find other business owners that you trust and can confide in. You'll discover that everyone has similar problems and that they can be solved.

7. Never stop exploring

Nothing in this world is black and white. Even black and white rarely are (look closely!)

You will never know everything. So, always keep looking, testing and learning. Whatever issues you may come up against, whilst you may not have the answer now, it is out there.

Personal strategy challenge two:
My business is a pain. How can I enjoy it again?

Challenge checklist	**Doing this!**	**Do more!**	**Start doing!**
1: Set congruent goals			
2: Keep track			
3: Choose what you do			
4: Check if success make you happy			
5: Ensure you aren't trying to be someone you're not			
6: Talk to others			
7: Never stop exploring			
TOTAL			

Transfer your totals to the table on Page 308.

Personal strategy challenge three: I have no time for myself and my family

Here are 7 things to try out. Give all of them a go and choose the ones that work best for you.

1. Work out exactly what you would do with any spare time

What exactly would you do with your family? What hobby or sport would you pick up again? Or start? What is the free time actually going to be for? Unless you put something concrete into its place, time will just expand again to fill the gaps.

2. Decide on how many hours of free time you need to generate

Even if you focus on pulling back one hour at a time, having a target to aim for will make the process easier.

Obviously, every week is different and it's hard to be too specific, but if you can create a target and a way to track your progress, then you can try different things out and see what does or doesn't work.

3. Block out personal time

Start with one or two hours here and there and then step it up at your pace. Eventually, you want to meet your target. Make sure you start with at least one hour. That first one is the hardest. When you've done it once, the second and third ones are just more of the same.

Then, treat that time as though it were your most important client.

4. Calculate what an hour of your personal time is worth

Think about doing something in your personal life that is really important. Really, really important. More important than that. Now, how much would a client have to pay you to cancel it?

You don't need to be too exact, but get a gut feel as to where your threshold will be. Now you can work out how much your personal time is worth to you.

5. Get ready to defend your territory

The life you are building is based on foundations. Your values, your lifestyle and, of course, your time. Any decent construction site would be fenced off and patrolled by guard dogs. So, only let people in who will help build your construction. If you think they might destroy it – set the dogs on them.

Are you clear about what you're protecting? Do you know where the threats are going to come from? Are you prepared to set the dogs on them?

6. Communicate your intentions

Use those who are currently losing out to bring some accountability to you.

Probably, your family. Tell them what you want to do and how you plan to do it. Give them permission to point out when it isn't working. And, of course, ask them to notice when it is.

7. Change your habits by disrupting your routines

What natural processes and inbuilt thought systems do you run through when you say yes to the wrong thing?

Find something in the process that happens every single time and put something in the way that will affect your train of thought. That will be enough to let in the new ideas and at least build them into your considerations.

For example, if you use the calendar on your phone, write out the number you came up with in Step 4), take a photo and set it as your screen lock image.

Now, every time you go to check their calendar, you'll remember that you need to think about defending your territory.

Personal strategy challenge three: I have no time for myself and my family

Challenge checklist	Doing this!	Do more!	Start doing!
1: Know what to do with spare time			
2: Decide on hours of free time needed			
3: Block out personal time			
4: Calculate value of an hour of personal time			
5: Get ready to defend your territory			
6: Communicate your intentions			
7: Change habits by disrupting routines			
TOTAL			

Transfer your totals to the table on Page 308.

Personal strategy challenge four: How can I improve my relationships?

We are social creatures and so good relationships are critical for personal satisfaction. Everything we do in life and business revolves around people.

Here are 7 things to try out. Give all of them a go and choose the ones that work best for you.

1. Assess the current position

Look at the different areas of your life and where you interact with people: Family, friends, staff, customers, suppliers.

There may be one or two specific individuals who you want to pick out due to their importance but otherwise you can stay with the general categories.

Have a think about how your relationship is with each group or person. Give it a score out of 10 – whatever works for you. Now you know where to focus your efforts

2. Decide what you want to it to look like

Start with the most important group or individual. What do you want to stop or to start happening? What do you want more or less of?

Work out what outcomes you want to create, then you can work out a plan.

3. Change yourself first

As well as being the easiest place to start, it is also the most powerful. Most people don't realise how much their own behaviour affects that of others. All they see is what the other person does.

Time to look in the mirror – and don't flinch: What are you doing to attract the bad relationship? How are you contributing to the situation? You will be, don't pretend otherwise. Get looking.

A good way to understand how people interact is to help others with their problems. It's always easier to spot the answers when other people have the issues, just make sure you learn from the process.

4. Temper your approach

Moving forwards, be more aware as to how you are interacting with others. It is very easy to make assumptions about what others are thinking or why they are doing things. Talk more. Ask questions more. Find out the real reasons.

We so often take it personally when things go against us. Take a moment to think about what is going on for them. Why should it be all about you?

Make sure your language is positive, whether you're talking to someone or about them. So often our off-the-cuff remarks come back to create bigger problems further down the line.

Run your relationships with these rules and you'll make great headway.

5. Reset or get rid

If you have a broken relationship, you need to make a decision.

If they are truly people that you want to keep in your life and have a better relationship with, then you will need to invest the time. Get a dialogue going, be honest and search out a way to get the relationship back on track.

If they are people who drain your energy, who contribute little to the bigger picture or are just going to take too much effort to bring back, then you've just got to let them go. Walking away from bad relationships can be one of the most liberating actions you can take.

6. Make deals

Good management of relationships is all about respecting each other's rules and boundaries and knowing which hat you're wearing at any particular time. For example, do not confuse your business owner hat and your parent hat.

Life, of course, never runs as planned, which means that there will be times when boundaries will need to be breached. The key thing is to not just plough on regardless, but to talk, negotiate and make deals. Need to work late one night? Then go out for dinner at the weekend.

It is, of course, critical that you honour your promises. Trust is hard won and easily lost.

7. Change the expectation

How we interact with others usually falls into a standard pattern of behaviour. Particularly around a contentious issue that can't be ignored. We know exactly how they'll react, our subsequent response and where the conversation will head. And nothing moves forwards.

If you want them to react differently, you need to break the cycle. Once the cycle has been established, you are expecting things to go a certain why and that is what happens. So, expect something different.

Before your next meeting, write down how you WANT them to react. Imagine them agreeing with your viewpoints and welcoming what you have to say. Now, when you go to meet them, your brain is envisioning a different situation and your reactions will be different. This will change how they respond and the cycle can start to shift.

It may take a while for the full effect to work through, but you must start somewhere.

Personal strategy challenge four: How can I improve my relationships?

Challenge checklist	Doing this!	Do more!	Start doing!
1: Assess the current position			
2: Decide what you want it to look like			
3: Change yourself first			
4: Temper your approach			
5: Reset or get rid			
6: Make deals			
7: Change the expectation			
TOTAL			

Transfer your totals to the table on Page 308.

Personal strategy challenge five: How can I improve my financial position?

We all kind of know that money isn't the be all and end all of everything. But it is important. Increasing income will come from the business side of things, but we need to know how to use it properly, regardless of how much we earn.

Here are 7 things to try out. Give all of them a go and choose the ones that work best for you.

1. Know the cost of personal goals

Setting targets is important in all areas, and money is no exception. You have already worked out what you want from life. So now work out, roughly, how much you need to make that happen.

The house you want, the car you like, the holidays you'll take. The memories you want to create. All of these have a financial implication. The figures might seem daunting, but it will be a sum for a period of time and, most importantly, it reinforces the purpose behind why you do what you do.

2. Treat money like precious water

Water is a vital commodity and should be treated with respect. And the proper way to manage water, like money, is by ensuring balance and flow.

Picture a reservoir. That is a lot of water and it took some time for it to fill up. It appears to be calm and static but, in fact, it is in a constant state of balance and flow. Water flows into the reservoir and it flows out at the same rate. If the flow in was too great, it would flood, If the flow out was too much, it would dry up. If you want to store more water, you increase the size of the reservoir.

So it is with money. You need to manage what comes in, what goes out and increase the amount that you're able to hold. This will require discipline but, once you get into the habit, it'll be the best discipline you have ever introduced.

3. Start saving

If you're the sort of person who spends all their money as soon as they get it, then you need to start disciplining yourself into saving money. To start with, any money that you are going to put to one side, comes out first. Before you spend any bills or buy any goods.

This may put you under pressure to start with, but, if you leave the saving element to last, there will never be anything left. Whereas, if you have less money to buy things with, then you can always find ways of getting around it.

You want to save for two reasons.

i. Specific projects – new car, new TV etc. Be specific, price them out and start building a pot.
ii. Passive income – saved money can be used to generate more money. It will start small, but over time it will grow. Never spend the pot.

Ideally, 10% of everything you earn should be moved into projects and 10% into savings. If that is too much, then start small and increase over time.

But start it.

4. Learn about better ways with money

Using money to create money is not that straightforward. Yes, you can put it in an ISA or high interest earning (remember that??) bank account, but that won't get you much back in the long run. You also need to understand yourself better. You will have some mental blocks on the amount of money you can earn. You need to understand these and remove them.

To increase the size of your reservoir, you're going to have to learn some new things. Better ways of earning money. Better ways of getting a return on it. Better ways of thinking. Hold some money back to use on yourself. This is the investment that will give you the biggest return.

5. Start spending

On the other hand, you need to make sure that you are not too tight on your spending. In our reservoir example, if the outlet is switched off, then the water essentially flows elsewhere. If all your time is focused on building a pot for the future, you won't take the time to enjoy life now. That will actually make it harder for you to earn the money you want, as it's a chore.

Pull out 10% of everything you earn and make sure you spend it EVERY month. Be as extravagant as you like, but make sure there is some reward for your efforts.

6. Give wisely

Part of the balance and flow is to make sure that you can help others with what you do. If you are in the situation where the more you earn, the more you can help others, then you will be incentivised to do better.

Give a proportion of everything you earn away to charity. Make it personal to you, something you care about. It might only be a small amount, but connect it to your income. Now, it's not all about you.

7. Make decisions based on now, not the future

Things will change over time and you're going to have to make lots of decisions on what you're going to do. When you're making a financial decision which is connected to your lifestyle, make sure you base it on the money you HAVE NOW.

Do not assume that income levels will stay as they are, that the promise someone made will be delivered. Potential income is not income.

This is the best way to make sure you never get into serious trouble.

Personal strategy challenge five:
How can I improve my financial position?

Challenge checklist	Doing this!	Do more!	Start doing!
1: Know the cost of personal goals			
2: Treat money like precious water			
3: Start saving			
4: Learn about better ways with money			
5: Start spending			
6: Give wisely			
7: Make decisions based on now, not future			
TOTAL			

Transfer your totals to the table on Page 308.

Personal strategy challenge six:
How can I become better at what I do?

Part of our ability to feel good about things is to feel confident in our own abilities. Our personal competency is therefore a fundamental area to focus on.

Here are 7 things to try out. Give all of them a go and choose the ones that work best for you.

1. Plan it out

Take a moment to think about which areas of your life you need to develop your skills in. Business, obviously. But also, things such as being a parent, managing your money, personal hobbies and any other area where you want to be the best you can.

Take another look at your personal and business goals and make sure they all fit together. Now throw you mind into the future and picture how you want to be in each of those areas. What would it look and feel like to be a fully actualised 'you'. Looking back to now, from the future, what path did you take to get here? What have you done to achieve this growth?

Time is an illusion. Our brains can't pick out any particular thought as being a moment in time. So, when we think about the future and what we've done to get there, our brains think that we've already done it. Which makes actually doing it a lot easier. From this future standpoint, plan out – roughly – what you want to do and in which areas. What are the key milestones that you want to achieve.

2. Take small steps

The key thing is not to try and leap straight to the end game. You do have time, so use it. Start off by taking small, easy to manage steps but heading in the right direction. Too much information will create overwhelm and you'll never even make a start.

Once you get going, it will be easier to continue.

3. Create headspace

Your brain is a muscle and learning is the equivalent of exercising that muscle. As well as being excellent for your long term mental health, it is also quite tiring. So, make sure that you are in the right frame of mind to start learning new information - otherwise it will be hard to do and hard to retain.

You need to find out what are the right times for you to work and what you need to do to keep up your energy levels.

It might be meditation: it could be eating the right foods. For some it is reserving the same time every day, for others it needs to be mixed up. Try different things, but reserve the time and give yourself the space.

4. Use both sides of the brain

A good training course will encourage you to use both the left and right sides of your brain as this way you will remember things more efficiently. When you are in control of your learning, make sure you do the same.

If all your time is spent in front of a computer, reading or making notes, then you need to tap into your more creative side. Draw diagrams, create cartoon images to represent the key points. The more outlandish they are the more you'll remember them.

Act out processes that you need to remember. Turn key messages into songs. None of it needs to be good – but it will increase your capacity to retain information.

5. Change your language

The language that we use affects the way we think. It is very easy, when learning new skills, to dismiss what we have done to date and focus on the end of the course.

I am training to be a ....

I going to become a ...

With the brain's inability to understand time, it will interpret both these phrases as: I am not ... Which will create resistance in our learning and can even make our brains reject what we have already learnt.

Our educational system has trained us in the concept of pass or fail. But this is not true learning. Learning is a gradual increase of knowledge and competency. There is no point where you 'are' or 'are not'. So, use phrases along the lines of:

"I am a ... and have increased my skills in the area of ...."

This will help cement your learnings.

6. Keep working on mindset

It is quite common for our educational focus to be on skills and fact-based learning. However, the most important area in which you can always be improving is around mindset. Mindset is the only reason why we are where we are and not where we want to be.

Always be looking for ways to challenge your beliefs, face your fears and look at the world in a different way. Mindset is everything.

7. Take action!

Learning without action is just a lot of expensive notes. Many people fall into the trap of moving from one course to another without actually consolidating what they have learnt.

As soon as you learn something that is beneficial to you, then start doing it. Straight away. Everything you learn is theory. It is only when you start testing and using this learning that it becomes reality.

Personal strategy challenge six:
How can I become better at what I do?

Challenge checklist	Doing this!	Do more!	Start doing!
1: Plan it out			
2: Take small steps			
3: Create headspace			
4: Use both sides of the brain			
5: Change your language			
6: Keep working on mindset			
7: Take action!			
TOTAL			

Transfer your totals to the table on Page 308.

Personal strategy challenge seven: How can I improve my health?

As our working and personal lives get busier, the first thing that seems to be sacrificed is our health.

Here are 7 things to try out. Give all of them a go and choose the ones that work best for you.

1. Decide you want to improve your health

You need to realise that your health is 100% your responsibility. The environment, our medical background, other people, are all influential but, at the end of the day what we do is down to us.

Improving our health is not about wishful thinking. It is about making a decision. That we want things to be better and we're going to do things differently. Until you do that, everything else is just playing to the crowd.

2. Look at the underlying reason

This is the hardest part of any health change. It isn't about the programme. It isn't about the diet. It's about the real reason why you're not listening to your body.

There will be a subconscious reason, a defence mechanism triggered by an emotional response to an old situation, that will be at the heart of the issue. Without getting clear on the fundamental issue, you're only temporarily treating symptoms.

You probably have an inkling as to what the reason is but, if you genuinely have no idea, then you need to speak to someone who is prepared to help you dig for it. A friend, a coach, a mindfulness practitioner, a doctor, a psychiatrist. It doesn't matter who, but it does matter that you do it.

3. Give yourself the time

Changing your routine around health and fitness requires time. Make that time available. Whether it's time in the morning to do exercise. Or time at the weekend to plan, shop and cook the right foods.

The practical starting point of any deterioration in health is when other priorities eat into the time we need. So, the practical starting point of getting back to health is to get that time back again.

See also Challenge number three of Personal Strategy.

4. Get an assessment

You need to truly understand what your starting point is. Get a medical assessment on all aspects on your health. If you can pay for a full blown private assessment, then do so. Otherwise, your local GP will be able to arrange one for you.

You will know some of the issues you have, but you won't know all of them, so it's best to get the big picture and where you fit into it.

5. Take small steps

New Year. Lent. Two popular times in the year where everyone decides to overhaul their attitude to health. Join the gym. Go on a diet. Cut out everything bad.

And it is always too much too quickly. So, unless you are medically advised to do otherwise, make small changes. Introduce a small amount of good habits. Remove some of the bad ones.

Don't try and do everything in one go. This is not a one-off exercise to solve a problem - it is a gradual shift towards a different way of life and should be managed accordingly.

6. Focus on actions

We do hold a lot of store in goals and targets, but getting too hung up on them can be detrimental.

If we set a target of reaching a certain weight by a certain date, and we don't achieve it – we feel bad and probably go and undo all the good work. If we do achieve it, we end up celebrating and, again, let the bad habits back in.

You definitely need to work out the direction you want to head in, but focus on the little actions that you can take every day. If, every day, you do a bit more exercise and eat a little more healthily, then the outcome will sort itself out.

7. Make it fun

Any change that feels like a chore will not be effective. So, find ways to make the process fun – or at least tolerable for the main part. This is often done by involving other people. Introducing a social element to the whole situation, as well as a bit of accountability.

Also, always look for the good things that you can do, rather than focusing on the bad things you can't. It is less about what you do and more about your attitude that will make the difference.

Personal strategy challenge seven: How can I improve my health?

Challenge checklist	Doing this!	Do more!	Start doing!
1: Decide you want to improve your health			
2: Look at the underlying reason			
3: Give yourself the time			
4: Get an assessment			
5: Take small steps			
6: Focus on actions			
7: Make it fun			
TOTAL			

Transfer your totals to the table on Page 308.

Part 2

Your business strategy Seven x7

Seven common challenges in business strategy

Your business strategy Seven x7

Seven common challenges in business strategy

Business strategy challenge one: I don't know where I'm going

It can be very easy to lose track as to where you are and where you're going. Many of us just start a business based on what we're good at and muddle along trying to do the best we can. Without a direction to head in, then muddling along is the best you can expect.

Here are 7 things to try out. Give all of them a go and choose the ones that work best for you.

1. **Look at your personal strategy**

Remember that you are in business for your own reasons. You're not there to line the pockets of others and you're certainly not doing it for the benefit of the business itself. It's not really about the money either. You can only truly say that you're in business to make money if you work for the Royal Mint.

The money you create, the time that you save, the prestige that you get are all there to support your personal ideals and plans. So, get your personal goals clear and make sure that your business strategy supports you as a person.

You run your business. Your business doesn't run you. Look at the seven personal strategy challenges listed further up and make sure you have conquered these as much as possible.

2. Work out where you are now

Take a moment to think about how things are right now. What is working well? What could do with some improvements? What's missing? What have you got too much of?

Be prepared to dig deep. Find and challenge a few assumptions. Are you really getting enough sales for the number of staff you have? Do things run as smoothly as you would like? Is there enough cash flowing around to allow you to do what you truly want?

Explore all aspects of your business and take stock of where things can be improved.

3. Decide what 'good' looks like

You know what you want to get out of the business personally. You know where the business currently is. So, decide where you want your business to move to, to get you what you want. If all your improvements came to fruition, how would things look? How would it feel? Start getting clear about what sort of business you want, how it operates, how it performs – and your role in the system.

You are developing a vision of the future, a direction in which to travel which can be communicated to all those that need to know it. The tighter you can get on the specifics, the easier it will be to develop a plan of action to get there and measure progress on the way.

4. Decide on who you're working with

You need to be clear on who you do your best work for and who you really want to work with. There is nothing worse than having a client who does nothing but cause disruptions, drain the energy of your team and then pay you late. Even if they are long-standing and high-paying, the negative impact of them being a client can often outweigh the benefit of the cash they bring in.

Work out who your ABCD clients are. These are the clients who you:

A. Really want to work with.
B. Are happy to work with.
C. Will work with, but only under certain conditions.
D. Won't work with.

This isn't just about the size of company and the industry. But also, their values, their ability to pay on time, how they behave towards you. They want to be people you enjoy working with.

Once you can define your ideal client, you can target your marketing to them, build filters into your process to test out their suitability and know when to disengage with them. You might even want to take a look at sacking a few of your existing clients.

5. Work out who you need to support you

Rule number one in any business is that you can't do it on your own. You will need a team of people to support you, both internally and externally.

In your vision of the perfect business, work out what positions you're going to need in the company. Strategy, operations and finance are the key three high level areas. Then work down from there. Do not forget the admin role. Vitally important to get that one right.

One person can do more than one role and staff is not a cost to be taken on lightly, so you're looking for a balance between low numbers and not overworking individuals – including yourself.

Then have a think about what your external team needs to be. Some of your internal roles could be outsourced. But you're also going to need a printer, a web and IT person, accountant etc. etc.

What will you be wanting from them, to support you? Not just their specific skills, but also the right type of person. People who fit your values and ones that you might be able to cross-refer with, so you can help each other on an extra level.

Your team needs to be built, and every member should only be there if they support you. Every employee should be a profit centre. Every supplier an investment.

It can take some time to get the right team, but it is the most vital ingredient in getting you to where you want to be. Hence, take your time in finding the right people.

6. Focus on the next 12 months

The overall picture of the company gives you a direction to head towards. In terms of detail, just focus on the next 12 months.

There is a lot of stall given to making 5 year plans, 10 year plans and so on, but you can't be that specific. A lot is going to change by then and anything you put down will be wasted. So, keep touch with the overall destination, but focus on what's just in front of you.

7. Monitor continually

How do you know how well things are progressing? Make sure you're able to keep track on progress between where you started and where you're heading.

There will be some very specific measures you can look at, such as sales and performance. Sometimes you just need to go through this process again and check that things 'feel' on track.

Make sure your overall direction is still correct. That what you want hasn't shifted over time. That way you can always adjust your course and keep yourself on track.

Business strategy challenge one: I don't know where I'm going

Challenge checklist	Doing this!	Do more!	Start doing!
1: Look at your personal strategy			
2: Work out where you are now			
3: Decide what 'good' looks like			
4: Decide on who you're working with			
5: Work out who you need to support you			
6: Focus on the next 12 months			
7: Monitor continually			
TOTAL			

Transfer your totals to the table on Page 309.

Business strategy challenge two: I don't really know who we are

To get the clients that you want, you need to know who you are, communicate your message and allow them to connect with you. Then everything gets a lot easier.

Here are 7 things to try out. Give all of them a go and choose the ones that work best for you.

1. Know your company's story

Why does your company exist? How did it come about? Why do the key people work there? What does it strive to do? How are you different from other companies in the same sector?

Everyone buys on an emotional level and if you can connect your company's story with the values of your ideal client, then you're going to find it easy working together. This is how you develop your corporate brand. It takes time to get right. You'll need to keep testing it and adjusting it. But get started.

2. Know your story

This is about you. There will be overlaps with your company's story, but you had a life before the business, and the business will have a life once you're gone. So, you need to conduct a similar exercise for yourself: Who are you? Where have you come from? Why do you do what you do? What is it that you do better than others? Why do you work with the people you work with? What do you do for your clients?

Start on it and keep working on it. This is how you develop your personal brand.

3. Know what you stand for

Your personal story and your company's story will all feed into what it is you stand for. You can sit down and pull together any other values that you feel are important to both you and the culture of your company.

But it goes further than that: What are the rules and boundaries that you're prepared to accept? What will you tolerate and what won't you tolerate? What is your view on late payments? Poor performance? On accuracy of content? Does everything need to be 100% correct – or is 80% good enough as long as the essential value is there?

Once again, this will be pulled together over time, but the clearer you can get as to what you stand for, the easier it will be for people to buy into you.

4. Do what you love

Your involvement in your business needs to be built around your passion. This is your business and you can design it however you like, so why do things you don't want to do? Do what you love. Anything else can be dealt with by someone else.

If that passion is the core of the business, then make sure that it runs throughout the entire company and all your external messages. If it is only part of it, then make sure that the other parts are covered by people who are equally passionate about what they are doing and find what links you all together.

If you don't enjoy your own business, you might as well get a job.

5. Make a difference

Whatever it is you do, it makes a difference to people's lives. Don't think that this needs to be some grand world changing event. Just changing a fuse for someone can make a difference to that person.

If you're purely supplying other businesses, think about how your product travels through the process and impacts on the end user. Be it peace of mind, time gained or money saved, all of these things make a difference to people.

As well as ensuring that it connects with who you are, you can use it to understand the true value of what you do – which will impact pricing – and work out new ways of making a difference – which will lead to new products.

Every business is formed around solving a problem. By making a difference. Be clear about what it is.

6. Create your culture

Your corporate culture is best defined as "how you do things".

Most cultures arise organically. Things are done a certain way, not for any real reason but...because that's just how it is. Whatever it is, it will all be driven from the top by you. If you fly off the handle at anyone who does the slightest thing wrong, then you will breed a culture of secrets and betrayal as everyone protects their own skin.

Here are a few suggestions of a better way of doing things.

Create a business where:

- the client is at the centre of everything you do.
- you focus on opportunities not problems.

- a mistake made is an excellent way to learn.
- everyone is human with weaknesses and flaws, so we help each other by being open and supportive.

Remember, you can start with it written down but it counts for nothing unless it is followed through. And it starts with you.

7. Enrol People

When you get clear about who you are, what you stand for, who you work for and how you do things, combined with a clear sense of the direction that you're heading in, then two things become a lot easier: You don't really sell any more. You don't really recruit any more. You enrol.

People will either want to work with you, or not, and either is ok. Only those on the same wavelength will buy into you. Then engagement will be about much more than just money and mere details.

When you work with clients you want to work with and employ people who want to work with you, life gets better and the business becomes more successful.

Business strategy challenge two: I don't really know who we are

Challenge checklist	Doing this!	Do more!	Start doing!
1: Know your company's story			
2: Know your story			
3: Know what you stand for			
4: Do what you love			
5: Make a difference			
6: Create your culture			
7: Enrol people			
TOTAL			

Transfer your totals to the table on Page 309

Business strategy challenge three: How do I stabilise?

For many people, the normal state of business is organised chaos. Never enough time, erratic cashflow and always fighting just to keep on top of things. It doesn't have to be like that.

Here are 7 things to try out. Give all of them a go and choose the ones that work best for you.

1. Slow down and create some thinking space

If you're constantly doing what you think you should be doing but not getting the right result, try doing the opposite. Counterintuitive as it may seem, instead of working harder and faster trying to get more and more work done, take a moment and slow down.

Blindly rushing about does not lead to creative thinking or effective performance. So, create some periods of calm where you can focus on resting your mind, redirecting the thought processes and start looking at changing the fundamental structure of how you work to enable you to produce more with less effort.

2. Work 'on' not 'in' your business

You're going to have to do a bit of both, but the more time you can spend thinking about strategy, direction, work processes and so on – instead of doing the work – the faster you'll be able to stabilise and grow your business.

Setting your business goals, planning on how to achieve them and checking you're still on course will be a fundamental part of this time. It will take a bit of time to shift from full-on working mode to thinking mode, but start to introduce things gradually and then increase it. But make a start.

Remember, Richard Branson doesn't actually fly the planes or drive the trains.

3. Establish focus/confidence/belief

A common reason for chaos is that we spend a lot of time focusing on the things that we can do – and not the things we should. This is because familiar things are easy and feel safe. At least we're achieving something.

However, if we focus on any area, even if it's something we're uncomfortable with, we will start to make progress with it. Then we'll gain confidence and then we'll have the belief that it can be done easily. So, just pick your battles effectively and choose where to focus your energies.

4. Focus on the 20%

A consequence of the 80/20 rule is that there will be a small number of key actions that you can take that will make a massive difference.

This is why you take time out - to identify these key steps and then apply focus in that area. If you can't see where to go, then ask someone from outside the business to give you a hand. They are more likely to see what you can't. Then you'll know where to start.

5. Gain momentum

Once you've got going, you need to make sure you keep going. The first few steps move you away from the immediate pain but, unless you underpin that work with real forward progress, you're most likely going to slip back to where you were before.

Increase the amount of time you spend on strategy, increase the number of people that get involved and keep communicating so it's not all left to one person. Keep monitoring things so that you can see where progress is being made and where more work is needed.

Quick fixes are just that. Long term solutions require long term projects.

6. Identify accountability

Use your team to help you, including your external team. But make sure they know what it is they need to do, why and what they are responsible for.

Communications need to be clear and open: Hold regular team meetings and ask everyone to report back on the specific things that they are responsible for. The more urgent the situation, the more meetings you need.

It is hard to hide when you've made a promise to the team and then have to report back on progress.

Remember, accountability is about making things happen, not necessarily doing them yourself, so the team should be encouraged to seek help when progress is at risk. The overall goal is more important than any individual becoming a hero.

7. Ask for help

Never feel like everything is down to you.

If you don't know what to do next, or are not sure which the right option to take is. If things aren't moving as fast as you would like. Ask for help! The biggest cause of business failure is down to people being too proud to ask for help early enough.

Business strategy challenge three: How do I stabilise?

Challenge checklist	**Doing this!**	**Do more!**	**Start doing!**
1: Slow down and create some thinking space			
2: Work 'on' not 'in' your business			
3: Establish focus/confidence/ belief			
4: Focus on the 20%			
5: Gain momentum			
6: Identify accountability			
7: Ask for help			
TOTAL			

Transfer your totals to the table on Page 309

Business strategy challenge four: How do I make more money?

Making money isn't all about increasing sales. Though that is, of course, one element.

Here are 7 things to try out. Give all of them a go and choose the ones that work best for you.

1. Focus on profit and cash, not turnover

The industry standard is to focus on increasing sales to generate more money, but that is only one factor in the equation. Shift your focus onto profit and cash and you'll be in a much stronger position.

Make sure you include the true cost of the business, which includes the actual time you spend in the business at a fair market rate. When you ignore your true cost you deem yourself worthless **and** end up doing most of the work. Find the true profit figure and work from that place.

2. Model the finances

Work with a management accountant or someone who knows their way around finances and spreadsheets to model your business.

You want to be able to easily calculate the impact of any changes you make. Increasing prices, reducing costs, adding a person here, removing a person there. You don't need to understand the specific numbers under the surface, but you do need to understand the impact of your actions.

3. Pay yourself first

So very often, the business owner pays out everyone else first and leaves themselves last to pick up what's left. This is certainly the easiest approach to take when funds are tight to avoid or minimise confrontation.
However, it is a false economy and, ironically, the reverse method has a more positive impact.

Set yourself a fair salary and pay yourself first. As counterintuitive as it seems, when you pay others out of what's left, then you are much more focused on selling more and doing deals. Also, you're valuing yourself, which will come through in your discussions with others.

The stronger you are personally, the more people you can help.

4. Set sales targets

Once you've modelled your business and worked out how much profit and cash you need to make to fulfil your business goals, you can play around with sale prices and cost figures.

Once you've settled on a set of assumptions to work with, you can work backwards to calculate what you need to do on the sales front. Things can probably be broken down into different categories, but you can now set targets which will deliver what you know you want.

5. Look at your customer base

One of the biggest contributors to poor cashflow is poor quality clients. If you have the wrong clients, you can't raise prices, it's hard to increase sales and collecting cash is a nightmare.

Decide on what clients you really do want, put filters into your sales process so that you only let the right ones in – which can actually increase demand for you – and start to change your client mix. You may even need to sack some of your existing clients.

Your clients hire you – but you also hire your clients, so hire wisely.

6. Look for added value products

Every customer who already buys from you has the greatest potential of buying more from you. However, instead of just selling them more of the same, sit down with your team and brainstorm new products.

Try to get into the head of your customer and find something that they would really value. Ideally you want to focus on products that have a high value to them and yet a low relative cost to you.

7. Develop a referral strategy

Do you have a referral strategy? I don't mean which networking organisations do you belong to. I mean what is your proactive approach to getting new customers from existing customers and associates?

If you don't have a specific and dependable system of generating referrals, then you need to develop one. If you don't have one, or have one that is erratic, then you need to start experimenting.

Here are three key starting points:

i. **Ask!** This is fundamental.
ii. **Financial incentive.** Basic but this works for some people.

iii. **Status incentive.** Make them look good. For example, let them give something of value to their clients that intrinsically includes a connection to you.

Time and money invested in finding referrals will give you a much better return than an investment in new sales, as a referral is much more likely to convert into a client. This is an area, therefore, that you should spend a lot of time experimenting in.

Business strategy challenge four: How do I make more money?

Challenge checklist	Doing this!	Do more!	Start doing!
1: Focus on profit and cash, not turnover			
2: Model the finances			
3: Pay yourself first			
4: Set sales targets			
5: Look at your customer base			
6: Look for added value products			
7: Develop a referral strategy			
TOTAL			

Transfer your totals to the table on Page 309

Business strategy challenge five: How do I grow?

Here are 7 things to try out. Give all of them a go and choose the ones that work best for you.

1. Be methodical

Any form of progress needs to be made step by step. When there is so much to do, where do you start? If it really isn't clear as to which area you should be starting in, then clearly it doesn't matter. Just start somewhere. The worst thing you can do is to do nothing.

Decide what to do first. Plan what you're going to do. Focus on the first step. Move forwards. Repeat that process, keeping in mind your end goals.

2. Balance time, team and money

Always keep one eye on the big picture. When you make changes in one area, it impacts another.

To find more time, you need a bigger team. To get a bigger team, you need more money. To make more money, you need more time. If you can't break this cycle in an obvious way, then small steps need to be made in every direction.

It's important that you understand how your business works. The key performance indicators and the growth levers. These are the things that will give you focus and traction when growing.

3. Introduce processes

Organic growth will only get you so far. If you truly want to scale up, you need to be introducing some systems and processes.

Look at your organisation and start off by imagining how things would operate if you weren't there. That will tell you where the problems are.

What processes and systems can you introduce to ensure things proceed effectively without you? Now remove other key staff and do the same. It will take time to develop things fully, but at least you'll know where you're heading.

4. Find blocks and remove them

Keep in mind the direction you want to be heading in. Make sure you look at every area of your business. Why don't you already have what you want? What's stopping you getting there?

Every barrier to progress is one of two things. It's either a genuine obstacle or it's an excuse. Analyse every barrier and be tough on yourself. Excuses can be ignored and every obstacle can be planned around.

5. Move as fast as you can manage

Slow change is very often no change. By the time you get around to fully implementing your plans, they become out of date and all that effort is wasted.

Break your big plans into smaller projects. Set timescales and deadlines, introduce accountability and regular reporting. The pace at which you can change will determine the pace at which your business grows.

6. Get the right team

Getting the right team can take time – and it should take time as the right team can be the difference between success and failure.

If you think about our 4 key areas – strategy, sales, delivery and finance – someone needs to be responsible for each area. Initially, one person can oversee more than one section but that is the model you want to head towards.

Work out in which areas the key people-priorities lie and focus on that area first. Surround yourself with people who are better than you. Any other strategy limits the ability of your company to grow.

7. Take the first step

It's all very well planning and strategising and working out on paper what you know you need to do. It all counts for nothing if you don't take action. And it all starts with the first step.

Don't wait until everything is perfect. Get started and work out the rest as you go along. It'll probably change anyway.

Business strategy challenge five: How do I grow?

Challenge checklist	Doing this!	Do more!	Start doing!
1: Be methodical			
2: Balance time, team and money			
3: Introduce processes			
4: Find blocks and remove them			
5: Move as fast as you can manage			
6: Get the right team			
7: Take the first step			
TOTAL			

Transfer your totals to the table on Page 309

Business strategy challenge six: How do I keep getting better?

Business growth is not about final destinations and is only achieved by continual improvement.

Here are 7 things to try out. Give all of them a go and choose the ones that work best for you.

1. Develop an improvement mindset

Anyone who thinks that they have learnt all that they need to learn, know all that they need to know and believe that no-one can teach them anything new, is setting themselves up for a big fall.

There is always something new to learn, a better way of doing things, a new method to try – however small. The ability of a business to improve is dictated by the ability of the owner to improve. So, become the person who is always looking for something new and business growth will follow.

2. Remove past assumptions

As Woolworths and BHS have demonstrated, relying on the past can be dangerous. Just because you've always done something, doesn't make it right. It doesn't necessarily make it wrong either.

As a start point, re-visit your existing business model and ensure you remove any assumptions. Only accept a point or a process if it can be justified based on evidence, not history. Always be on the look-out for ways of undertaking established processes more productively.

3. Remove future assumptions

How many of your future plans are based on things staying the same as they are now? The customer base, the economic landscape, the level of demand?

Every future projection is based on assumptions, but many of these will be based on even bigger ones. Drill down into what you're basing your forecasts on and make sure you understand the repercussions of change.

4. Use your team

Development of your company doesn't have to rest solely on your shoulders. Use your team to help the business to develop and innovate. Remember, those doing the work will have a much better idea on how to improve small details.

Look to reward innovation and make sure it applies throughout the process. From sales and manufacturing through to administration. A small saving can be a big earner.

5. Keep track of the numbers

The numbers will always tell you the truth. If you want to know how to get better, where to focus your efforts and to track the level of those improvements, then you need to keep track of the numbers.

As a business owner, you only need the high-level figures that inform you of what you need. Get someone else to look at the detail. With clear strategic targets and the right measures, you can manage whatever growth you want.

6. Keep in touch with the customer

You need to be fully up to speed with what is going on in your market place, so, as well as the usual customer relationship side of things, it's important you keep in touch with your customers to keep your finger on the pulse.

They will provide you with news and updates and you can also use them as a research tool by trying out new ideas on them. Your business is only as strong as your market, so always ask your market what it wants.

7. Use third parties

We don't know what we don't know. Which means our ability to come up with new ideas is always restricted by our existing level of knowledge.

This reinforces the importance of using people outside of your business to help generate new ideas and areas of innovation. By bringing in a new dimension, the results can be much greater than you could possibly believe.

Business strategy challenge six: How do I keep getting better?

Challenge checklist	Doing this!	Do more!	Start doing!
1: Develop an improvement mindset			
2: Remove past assumptions			
3: Remove future assumptions			
4: Use your team			
5: Keep track of the numbers			
6: Keep in touch with the customer			
7: Use third parties			
TOTAL			

Transfer your totals to the table on Page 309

Business strategy challenge seven: How do I get out?

Many business owners just do what they do without having an exit strategy in mind. Yet this is the one guarantee of any business: at some point, you won't be there.

Here are 7 things to try out. Give all of them a go and choose the ones that work best for you.

1. Establish your destination

You may be very early in your business cycle, but one eye on how you want to exit is always worth having.

- Do you want to create a business of value and then sell it?
- Do you have family that you hope will take over its running?
- Or is your business built around you and, as you wind down, so does the business?

It doesn't matter which route you want to go down, just knowing the destination will determine what you do.

2. Define what structure your business needs

Knowing which route you want to go down determines the structure that your business needs to have.

At the end of the day, if you want the business to continue in some capacity without you in it, then it will need to be self-sufficient. Take some time to work out what your business is going to have to look like based on where you want it to end up.

3. Set a value for your business

If the value of the business is important to you – i.e. a sale or transfer to family, then you need to have a figure in mind to work towards. How much will you want to sell it for?

Valuations of businesses can be complex, with many variables to take into account, but you can easily get an indicative rule of thumb if you know what to look for. Ask your accountant about other companies in your industry or find someone who has sold their business recently. Whether valuation is based on profit, turnover or asset levels, find a method you understand and work out what your business needs to look like.

For example, if value is approximately 3 times turnover and you want to sell it for £1m, then you know you need turnover of around £350k.

Make sure that you include a fair market value for your salary, regardless of what you actually take. Otherwise you'll distort the figures.

4. Create a plan

Now you have an end game to head for, make sure you know what the turnover and profit figures need to be and develop a growth plan to get to that target.

Create milestones and interim steps that will get you there and then focus on the first one only. Once you achieve it you can review the situation, in case something has changed, and then go again.

5. Sack yourself

There will be a point when you're no longer involved in the business, so your job is to enable the 'possibility' of that happening as quickly as possible.

In other words, what do you need to do with the business so that you are able to sack yourself (if you so wish!)?

Now you can start thinking about succession plans. Remember that succession plans are about ability, not availability. And think two or three steps ahead. If one person moves up, that creates gaps below. Who will fill those gaps?

Ultimately, a business that runs without the owner is a true business.

6. Create the necessary processes

Once you've envisioned a business without you in it, you can start developing the processes you need to allow it to happen.

McDonald's are a good example of a company where everything is fully systematised: the processes; the jobs; and the training. Everyone knows exactly what they're doing and how to do it.

It takes a lot of work to get there, so that's why you need to start some time in advance.

7. Have a retirement plan

Remember to develop a personal strategy around exiting your business. The closer you get, the more important it is. Whatever you do, don't just stop working one day, as you'll quickly go insane.

Start increasing the amount of time you spend away from work. Start to develop ideas about how you want to spend your free time and start doing it. Even if it's starting a new business, get it under way and transition yourself out, rather that step out.

Business strategy challenge seven: How do I get out?

Challenge checklist	Doing this!	Do more!	Start doing!
1: Establish your destination			
2: Define what structure your business needs			
3: Set a value for your business			
4: Create a plan			
5: Sack yourself			
6: Create the necessary processes			
7: Have a retirement plan			
TOTAL			

Personal and business strategy challenges seven x7: What next?

So, we have now given you two sets of seven x7 points to help you to navigate through the key personal and business challenges that you are likely to face in future. That's just under 100 different points in total! Use the checklist summaries at the end of each section to look back and see the key ones you need to work on, given your specific circumstances right now.

Transfer the totals through to the summary tables at the end, if that helps.

Part 3

Your sales strategy Seven x7

Seven common challenges in sales strategy

Your sales strategy Seven x7

Seven common challenges in sales strategy

As with the personal and the business strategy, here are seven key areas of sales strategy, each with 7 points to work on. There are two ways to achieve more profit. One is to spend less and the other is to sell more. This series of strategies is about how to generate more revenue from sales.

You are looking for quick wins and in our experience, they are always there. Please note that we interchange the words products and services throughout. These words denote whatever it is that you sell to your clients.

Sales strategy challenge one:
How can I increase my profits by selling more?

Here are 7 things to try and do. Try them out and see if they fit. Then choose the ones that work best for you.

1. **Decide how much sales revenue you want**

Get clear exactly how much extra sales you want and by when. Check your numbers and make sure that you can deliver this amount of extra sales, and that you can manage any extra cash-flow requirements.

Then drill down to establish exactly how this sales increase looks, in terms of existing and new customers, and new products and services. Use the "Five Ways to Improve Profit" model explained in Point 6 to help you calculate:

- How many extra sales leads you will need to generate.
- What your conversion rate for these needs to be.

- How many transactions you need from each customer. The average £ value sales you will need from each sale.
- Your total sales revenue.
- The margin you expect to gain from each sale.
- Your expected profit.

2. Discuss and agree this with your internal team

Put this information on your agenda to discuss and agree with everyone on your team.
Break the overall task down into what it means to each individual and team. Don't let them guess how they may be affected by these changes. Explain fully what you expect will occur.

But make sure that you tell them how you will be there for them if they require any help to complete their personal outcomes. Your job is to create belief that the outcomes can and will be achieved by everyone. Remember that TEAM stands for: **T**ogether **E**veryone **A**chieves **M**ore.

Take time to explain the changes to them in personal terms. "What's In It For Me?" (WIIFM). How much better they and everyone else will be. Discuss in terms of increased job security, bonuses, higher salaries, affording to employ more staff etc. You must take the time and effort to get them on the bus. 100% committed to the outcomes. Total belief it will be done.

3. Explore your main alternatives to increase revenue

In level of increasing risk these are:

a) Sell more of the existing products to the same customers
b) Sell some new products to the same customers
c) Sell existing products to different customers
d) Sell new products to different customers

The risk here is the amount of money and resources you may use up before you get the sales increase you require.

Depending upon the length of your sales cycle, the quickest wins are not usually to be had from (c) and (d) above. These involve finding new customers and persuading them to buy from you. This takes time and effort. But should be part of your long-term growth strategy.

Quick wins can be from (a) and (b) where you already have a sound relationship with your present customers. There are usually opportunities for long term growth in these strategies, but this may depend upon how cost effectively you can service increased demand for these products.

4. Increase your prices

A very quick way to increase your profits without the added costs of selling more is just to increase your prices. You may attach significant risk to doing this. But the potential upside makes this strategy well worth investigating. You may be more comfortable doing this in small increments, a few customers at a time rather than everyone at once.

Do not be afraid to test your prices.

The next time you go shopping, note the prices you pay for certain specific products. Then price check these over subsequent weeks and months. Note how the retailer tests prices by increasing them gradually until the demand drops. And then adjusts either their price or the product to arrive at the price where the demand equals the number of products they want to sell.

If you do not test your prices, you lose this huge opportunity to improve your profits.

And you also set yourself up for a longer-term challenge. This occurs when your costs rise and you have no choice but to increase your prices. At this point you may have to increase your prices by 10% or more when the Retail Price Index (RPI) is only 2% or 3%.

You then need to explain why you are increasing your prices well above the RPI.

Much better to review your prices at a minimum every year and increase them by a small amount. Your customers probably will not notice, and you have the choice whether you draw their attention to this increase or not.
There are usually quick wins to be had by examining your prices. If you sense this opportunity, get started on it today!

5. Match your chosen customer segment with your sales process

Look at your selling numbers and apply the 80/20 rule to establish any effects, where a minority of customers or products generate a disproportionately high profit. For example, you may note that 20% of your customers or products produce 80% of your profit. It may not be exactly 20/80 but there will be this likely level of disproportion. Just focus your investigation on finding the highest possible disproportional effect within your products and/or customers and the profit they generate.

You are looking for exactly where to focus your limited resources to produce the maximum effect on your profits. Once you have done this, focus all your efforts on this defined segment of customers and/or products or services.

The next stage is to write down the steps in your sales system that you use to get sales with these clients:

These will be similar to:

- Prospecting
- Building rapport
- Identifying customer needs
- Presenting your solution
- Answering client objections
- Closing the sale

If relevant add the next steps:

- Getting re-sales
- Asking for referrals

Then look for ways to lubricate each step throughout your sales process to ensure that you attract and convert as many of these customers as possible.
Calculate the numbers throughout this process, and insert these into the ***Five ways to improve profit*** model below. This helps you to identify any resistance throughout your sales process. You can then focus on reducing the friction at this step.

To make your sales process most efficient, begin with the biggest resistance and then work through each subsequent resistance. Gradually improving your sales process for these customers and products. Then pick the next segment on which to focus your attention and resources.

6. Use The 5 Ways to Improve Profits

Use the following model to check through each of your sales processes. At each stage ask yourself if there is any opportunity to improve your outcomes and create extra profits.

The 5 Ways to Improve Profits

1) No. of Leads
x
2) % Conversion Rate = No of Customers
x
3) No. of Transactions
x
4) Average £ Sale = Sales Revenue
x
5) Margin = PROFIT

7. Be coherent with: market – media – message

You may find it useful to consider the cohesion between each of your market segments, the media through which you communicate to each segment, and the message that you communicate through each media.

When you have selected the market segment that will produce the biggest return from the least effort, do take the time to check for this cohesion. There is not usually much opportunity to quickly establish a new media to talk to your market. But there is often a good opportunity to refine and improve the message you are communicating to your prospects.

The first step is to look at all your marketing communication with your chosen segment and consider:

- Does each piece communicate the same message?

- Does every word that you write and speak tell exactly the story that you want to tell?
- When you check all your printed material, your online material, your sales presentation and delivery scripts – are these giving a consistent message?
- Is there something important you are not telling your clients?
- Could there be something you can do to tell a stronger, clearer story?
- Is this worth checking out with a marketing specialist?

Make sure that you are telling the very best story about your offers. If not, then you are not producing the level of sales that you could because your communication process is not working optimally.

We find that most businesses do not communicate their story as effectively as possible. Once you improve this it has a huge impact on your sales.

Sales strategy challenge one:
How can I increase my profits by selling more?

Strategy checklist	Doing this!	Do more!	Start doing!
1: Decide how much sales revenue you want			
2: Discuss and agree this with your internal team			
3: Explore your main alternatives to increase revenue			
4: Increase your prices			
5: Match your customers with your sales process			
6: Use the 5 Ways to Improve Profits			
7: Be coherent with market – media - message			
TOTAL			

Transfer your totals to the table on Page 310

Sales strategy challenge two:
How to improve your marketing and selling by testing and measuring

We were once asked by a workshop attendee, "Is there anything in marketing and selling that is guaranteed to work every time?" We told them that we have discovered only one - testing and measuring (T&M).

Because T&M can be done at minimal cost, it will always lead to improved decision making, and will often provide insights which are way outside of normal intuition. Also, T&M has no opinions, makes no judgements, has no ego, no ambiguity and will create cohesion within your team: a terrific payback for taking a little time and trouble.

For further comments about T&M, refer back to our piece at the beginning of the book, **'A word or two around testing and measuring'.**

Here are 7 things to think and do. Try them out and see if they fit. Then choose the ones that work best for you.

1. Write down your selling process for each of your market segments

This starts to get you into the mind-set for analysis. Gets you thinking about exactly how you perform these processes.

One page for each process is good enough. Or just focus on those processes where you sense that you have a challenge, or a missed opportunity.

The next stage is to write down the steps in your sales system that you use to get sales with these clients. You may have already done this as part of **Sales strategy one**, above

These will be similar to:

- Prospecting
- Building rapport
- Identifying customer needs
- Presenting your solution
- Answering client objections
- Closing the sale

If relevant add the next steps:

- Getting re-sales
- Asking for referrals

Then write underneath each heading exactly what you do at that stage of the process:

- How do you find new prospects?
- How do you build rapport and build trust with your clients?
- How do you answer client objections?
- How do you close the sale?

This exercise will get you thinking about which stages give you the most challenges. Start with these and then look for ways to improve them. Make sure that you test and measure at each change to create gradual improvements throughout your selling processes.

2. **Write down your delivery processes for each of your market segments**

By thinking and writing about how you perform these processes, you are getting into the right mind-set to test and measure. Take this opportunity to stop and capture exactly what you do to deliver your product or service.

One page for each process is good enough. Or just focus on those processes where you sense that you have a challenge, or a missed opportunity. Remember that every interaction with your customer is an opportunity to improve your relationship with them.

Consider your effectiveness at every touch point with your customers. At each touch point, are you doing the very best that you can for your client?

For example:

- Do you use telephone scripts every time you or your staff talk with your clients?
- As you serve your clients do you have a prepared list of other products or services you could offer them?
- Do you have an established follow up process after delivery?

Check through your delivery system. Are there any steps that you could enhance for the benefit of your customers? Do you notice any other ways that you could help your customers and add even more value to the transaction?

Apply test and measure to each change before you make that a wholesale change. In this way, you will create gradual improvements throughout your delivery processes and build a stronger bond with your clients.

3. Apply 80/20 to your selling and delivery processes

You may already have experienced some insights from writing down your selling and delivery processes. Now it's time to go deeper and discover your focus for action.

For now, focus on your sales and marketing numbers. Look for disproportionate effects between inputs and outputs:

- Who are your 20% of customers who contribute 80% of your overall profit?
- Which are the 20% of your products or services that contribute 80% of your overall profit?

Then look through the 80% of customers who contribute only 20% of your profit. Are there any of these where you are in fact losing money? Any that you should immediately increase prices? Any that you must stop dealing with?

And look through the 80% of your products that contribute only 20% of your profit. Can you increase any of their prices? Do you need to stop supplying these products?

Keep digging until your focus becomes clear. Which selling and delivery processes are not producing an adequate return on resources? Can you shorten these to make them cheaper to perform?

Consider dropping certain products or customers to free up resources that can be better applied on more profitable customers, products and services and produce more profit for your business.

By looking first at the selling and delivery processes and then at the products and services that you supply using these processes, you will get a good awareness of where you can make improvements to profitability.

Use this analysis to make sure you start with the biggest opportunity to create a quick win. Exploit this and then move to the next biggest and so on.

4. **Identify qualitative and quantitative measurements**

Start with the quantitative measures as they are easier to define, analyse, and communicate. But as you work through your systems, products, services and customers take every opportunity to note any qualitative elements.

Then ask yourself "What if we could do this for our customers?" And seek clarity on what impact this would have on your business.

Think like Einstein:

*"Not everything that **COUNTS** can be counted, and not **EVERYTHING THAT CAN BE COUNTED COUNTS**"*

Identifying and improving the qualitative elements of your processes can produce big effects upon sales. However, qualitative improvements do not tend to just drop into your lap. Most are discovered through sticking at these processes. But when you find them, it is a good day for you and your business.

5. Identify key quantitative and qualitative Key Performance Numbers (KPNs)

Most businesses have no fast measure of their day-to-day activities. Mostly they are looking at historical figures that are usually weeks if not months old. These are usually accurate, but not up-to-date enough to correctly inform management decisions. Something can be going out of kilter and it is often some time before this is picked up.

A way to address this issue is to find certain Key Performance Numbers (KPN). This is the term that we use because they are simple numbers and not Key Performance Indicators (KPIs), which can be more complex to calculate, manage and administer.

A typical KPN for a small business could be the number of hours they have billed, today, this week, this month. This is easily accessible from their accounts package and gives a real-time measure of where they are by day, week etc.

Comparing the number of hours billed today with another KPN such as Daily Break Even Point puts the business manager in full knowledge of the urgency of his actions. For a business that generates a large volume of transactions such as a retail outlet, they usually have a financial package that summarises every transaction through every till. In that way, they can see their total daily sales, and often how sales are progressing throughout the day. In this example the KPN would be daily sales.

Finding your KPNs is important to your business success because they allow you to easily measure your day-to-day performance in real time. The sum of your day-to-day performances add up to whether you achieve your monthly, yearly, etc. objectives.

Typical businesses do not need any more than 4 to 6 KPNs. But you do need to know the metrics used to calculate these, so that you can check for what is happening underneath each KPN when the KPN is off track. If you are uncomfortable finding your KPNs. we suggest that you discuss this with your accountant and ask them to help.

Qualitative KPNs are trickier to establish and measure, as they are inevitably more subjective that quantitative KPNs. Think about ways in which people might say that they feel good about dealing with or working in your business. Then try to formulate a way of expressing and measuring this. A good example of a qualitative KPN could be the number of ways that your team can manage to say "Thank you for your business" to your customers.

6. Identify and highlight weakest spots first and sort

Earlier, we discussed how to locate fast and easy ways to focus your efforts to make improvements. You are looking for fast and easy ways to measure your results. BUT, do not drop into paralysis by analysis.

Keep your measuring to the minimum, by finding and focusing on only those KPNs that produce your greatest returns. Those KPNs that are critical for managing and improving your current business performance.

Keep these KPNs as up-to-date as possible. Bring them to the attention of you and your team. Get them in your face, so that you maintain your focus on these until they reach your targets. Then shift your attention to the next KPN, and so on. Remember the maxim from Peter Drucker:

"What gets measured gets managed"

7. Ask for help!

Your accountant is an obvious first ask. By performing the type of analysis outlined above you will be more informed to provide the focus for them and explain exactly what you are looking to manage.

Also, they will use less time and their bill will be cheaper if you do some of the work yourself and then ask them the right questions.

Stay on the specific areas that you have discovered where you require their help to find your KPNs. Do not allow them to bamboozle you with an overwhelm of management numbers.

Make sure that you keep things simple. You want fast information that is cheap to produce.

And the easier this information is to understand, the more use you will make of it.

If you are a business owner who is less than comfortable with finance and numbers, I recommend that you consider asking your accountant to build the financial model for your business with your KPN calculations included. This allows them to easily and quickly help you with deeper analysis if your KPNs go off track. They will be able to help you over the telephone while looking at your financial model.

Sales strategy challenge two:
How to improve your marketing and selling by testing and measuring

Strategy checklist	**Doing this!**	**Do more!**	**Start doing!**
1: Write down your selling processes			
2: Write down your delivery processes			
3: Apply 80/20 to sales and deliveries			
4: Identify qualitative and quantitative measures			
5: Identify KPNs			
6: Identify and sort weak spots			
7: Ask for help!			
TOTAL			

Transfer your totals to the table on Page 310

Sales strategy challenge three: How to improve margins and profits… fast

There are usually some quicks wins to be had. Small changes in your selling or marketing that yield fast profits. These do not need to be big wins, as they multiply up. A 2% improvement in 10 areas yields 23% overall improvement. And a 2% improvement in 20 areas yields a 64% overall improvement.

Depending upon the complexity of your business there can be many places to find these marginal improvements. Here are 7 things to try and do. Try them out and see if they fit. Then choose the ones that work best for you.

1. Know the impact of your sales cycle

The time taken for any improvements depends upon the duration of your sales cycle. This is the time it takes for you to convert your prospects into buying customers. The longer this process, the more time is needed for you see any improvements. As you respond to your market with better offers, know the time it takes for your market to say "Yes we'll buy that".

Look for ways to shorten your sales cycle. For example:

You may visit your prospect and then send them a proposal to consider and then follow up by telephone a week later after they have had time to study it. Consider speeding this up by writing and sending a shorter, less complex proposal based on their needs and not the full complexity that you need to install the proposal. Then follow up within 2 days. Discuss the short proposal and then adjust the more complex proposal that you have kept with you.

Then call in to talk them through this using your complex proposal. This will both shorten your sales process and improve your conversion rate. Firstly, you have built greater momentum and speed into the sales process, and secondly, you have avoided the possibility of giving your prospect the time to use your complex proposal to talk to your competitors. Can you shorten your sales process and speed it up?

2. Obtain quick wins from price discounting

Discount pricing can produce the quickest market response. January sales and other seasonal offers are used extensively in the retail sector. These were originally just for selling off old stock before re-stocking, but they have now become far more than that, with retailers buying in specific lines to sell in their seasonal sales. These can be used to improve footfall, with the objective of picking up sales from other products while the customer buys sale items.

So, there is always a clear purpose and strategy behind retail seasonal sales.

Likewise, you should never use discount pricing without being totally clear of your strategy. You may just be selling off old or slow moving stock items to produce cash.

You may package up a number of your products or services into a bundle and sell these for an overall discount. You may have bought these products or services at a discount just for this purpose. Whatever the version of a sale that you run with, the idea is to produce an offer that the prospect looks at and quickly decides, "Yes I'll have that".

But, beware of applying simple price discounts to your normal products and services. This is because, depending upon your gross margin per sale, as you discount your price by 10%, you may have to sell significantly more products to produce a bigger total profit.

So, always do your numbers before using discount pricing. Make NO exceptions to this and you will use discounting to gain quick wins by moving slow or old stock, attracting new clients, testing the attraction of your product or service packages, and creating more margin and profits.

There are various notes on pricing throughout this book for you to pick up on and use.

3. Check your current prices

Many business owners do not adjust their prices regularly. Even as their input costs increase over time. This results in their margin being eroded because their prices have become too low.

Check the margins on all your products and services. Focus on those where the margin is too low and adjust these immediately. If you feel that the gap is too big to increase your price all at once to where it should be, then spread the rise over two or three increases. But start right away. It is cash straight down to your bottom line.

Consider an overall price increase across your whole range of products and services. It's better to make small adjustments more frequently than having to sell a large increase sometime in the future.

Many businesses do not even inform their clients they have increased prices. They just add 2% or 3% onto their prices every year or biannually. Have you scrutinised the pattern of pricing from all your suppliers??

If you feel your customers will go elsewhere if you increase your prices, then make sure that you do your numbers first, to find the lowest margin products. And if necessary test your new prices on a few customers to start with before rolling the increases out to all your clients.

4. **Increase profits by making quick changes to your 5 Ways**

Revisit the Five Ways to Improve Profit – this is detailed in point 6 in **Sales strategy one.**

Starting with your high profit products or services, plot your numbers into this formula and look for quick ways to make your process increase your numbers of customers, deliver more sales, margin and profit:

1) No. of Leads
x
2) % Conversion Rate = No of Customers
x
3) No of Transactions
x
4) Average £ Sale = Sales Revenue
x
5) Margin = PROFIT

Do this by looking for quick ways to increase your number of leads. Maybe make some adjustments to your prices and the perceived value of your offers to encourage more prospects to buy. Possibly adjust your marketing message or your marketing spend to generate more leads.

Is your conversion rate for each product and service consistent across all your offers? If not, investigate why not. Can you lubricate your selling and delivery processes? Can you spot any obvious resistance in your conversion processes?

Check whether your customers are returning as often as you would expect. Compare the number of transaction with the length of your sales process. Perhaps you can find ways to encourage them to return.

For example: A restaurant may create a customer information list and then send special offers to different customers on birthdays, anniversaries, etc. to tempt them to re-visit. Or may just send quick offers by text message to persuade clients to visit at quiet times.

As you sell your product and your customer says "Yes", is there anything else you could have sold them at the same time? If there is, then create lists of these added products to remind you to ask if they need these extras. These add-on products are a huge source of extra revenue, because your first sale has covered all your costs of acquiring that customer. Therefore, any extra sales value goes straight to your bottom line.

Make regular checks on your margins for every product. Input costs are always creeping up and these gradually erode your margin. Make your % margin a KPN that you check weekly or at least monthly to make sure it remains on track.

Also, make your profit a KPN that you check regularly.
Make sure that when you see a fall in your margin and profit numbers, that you immediately examine why this has occurred. Always stay on top of your numbers. They create money in the bank that allows your business to grow and prosper.

Regularly look at what you do at every step of this process. Can anything be quickly and easily adjusted to make a positive change to your 5 Ways numbers?

5. Quickly examine each step of your marketing, selling and delivery systems

Focus your efforts here by firstly applying 80/20 analysis to find disproportionate profits being generated from a few of your products or customers.
Then write out your marketing, selling and delivery processes for these products.

- Can you see any obvious bottlenecks or areas of resistance?
- Are your customers dealt with smoothly throughout each process?
- Are there any opportunities for you to make quick and easy adjustments to your marketing process to bring in more sales leads?
- Where can you step up your marketing efforts to increase your number of leads for these highly profitable products or services?

Look at each individual marketing process that produces your leads. Are you wasting money because any particular process has become a cost and not an investment?

Check for any marketing process that was producing high quality leads of acceptable cost that has slipped and now is not so attractive. Can you switch money and resources from this onto other marketing processes that still produce an acceptable return on your investment?

Also, focus on each selling process for these chosen products. Are the 5 Ways to Improve Profit numbers showing what you would expect? Are there any obvious bottlenecks that are reducing the overall efficiency of your sales process?

Examine your delivery processes in the same way, step by step. Remember that small improvements add up and they all end up in your bottom line profit.

6. Quickly examine your products and services

Once more, focus your efforts by using 80/20 analysis to find those products or services that are producing a disproportionate share of profits. Then prioritise and work through each of these offers.

- Is there any opportunity to increase your average sale value?
- Is there anything that you now supply for free that you could charge for?
- Can you add extra value to individual offers and charge more?
- Could you make a package of goods or services that is more attractive to these buyers, that increases your overall profit per sale?

Consider our earlier example: If you visit your prospect and then send them a proposal to study, could you charge them for preparing a complex proposal? You consult with them on this until it matches their exact budget and technical requirements. Then when they give you their business, you may discount this charge from your final invoice for the work.

Where possible, always avoid doing free work for clients to get their business. Free is a strategic tool that gets you the interest of your prospect. If you do "Free" beware of giving away your skills and knowledge to prospects who take and take but do not give you what you want from them.

If you are in a business where you buy and sell items, are there any deals that you can do with your suppliers to increase your profits and fulfil their objectives? These may be new or improved product introductions, or stock they want to clear etc.

Keep looking for quick ways to improve your margins: Increase prices; reduce your costs for marketing, selling and delivery; reduce client acquisition costs; and so on.

I guarantee you will discover enough extra profit to make a good return on your time and effort.

7. Stay focused

Make this evaluation manageable by focusing only on certain key parts of your products or services. Pick one product/service or customer segment and stay on this one until you have improved it as much as practicable.

This stops you getting into paralysis by analysis, where you generate too much information to make informed decisions. And keeping focus will keep you on track to then find many positive incremental improvements.

Keep your effort focused on achieving quick and easy wins. They are always there. But be prepared to dig to find them.

Sales strategy challenge three: How to improve margins and profits... fast

Strategy checklist	Doing this!	Do more!	Start doing!
1: Know the impact of your sales cycle			
2: Obtain quick wins from price discounting			
3: Check your current prices			
4: Increase profits by changing the 5 Ways			
5: Examine your marketing, selling and delivery			
6: Examine your products and services			
7: Stay focused			
TOTAL			

Transfer your totals to the table on Page 310

Sales strategy challenge four: How to use marketing to improve your profits

There are usually some quick wins to be discovered within your marketing processes. But even if you do not immediately discover them, there is no harm in spending a little time just reconsidering your activities.

Here we explain some practical ways that can help you to focus and then consider your marketing activities.

Here are 7 things to try and do. Try them out and see if they fit. Then choose the ones that work best for you.

1. Focus your scarce resources

Every business only has limited marketing and sales resources. Many businesses spread these too thinly over their marketing and sales processes. And over too many product and customer segments. This quickly uses up the available resources, but produces no appreciable results. There is not enough measurable outcome to build upon to make further gains by testing and measuring.

Therefore, do not dissipate your scarce resources. Instead, use 80/20 or similar, to analyse where you can focus your resources to create a disproportionate result. By focusing your resources as tightly as possible, you will produce a definable result that you can probably test and measure.

You can then invest your resources to generate improvements until your testing and measuring shows that you have taken your current marketing strategies as far as is practicable. Then you switch your resources to your next area of focus.

2. Use 80/20 analysis to find your focus

You may already know those customers and products that are your most profitable. But when you apply actual numbers to these thoughts, then you have started on a powerful strategy that you can use to improve your results.
Using 80/20 analysis, start with those customers and product segments that you think are your most profitable, and check exactly how disproportionately profitable they actually are.

Then move onto the rest of your customers and products to discover which of these are yielding disproportionate results. You may find some surprises as you look for:

- Customers who produce high profits with low sales and delivery costs.
- Customers who produce low profits with high sales and delivery costs.
- Products that produce high profits with low sales and delivery costs.
- Products that produce low profits high sales and delivery costs.

Then decide on which products, services and customers you will focus your marketing and sales resources. Be clear whether you can reach and satisfy more customers within your chosen customer segment. Also, check that you have the resources to sell and deliver the products and services which you have shown will yield disproportionate results.

Turn your attention to those customers, products and services that cost you most to market, sell and deliver, but yield poor profitability. Perhaps review and increase your prices here. But whatever you do, put more effort where you will gain more profit and less effort where you have gained least profit.

In this way, can use the same overall resources, but produce far greater profits. Do not stop this work until you find the easiest, fastest, biggest selling returns from using your limited resources.

3. Revisit your unique selling proposition (USP)

A USP is defined as:

The factor or consideration presented by a seller as the reason that one product or service is different from and better than that of the competition.

There is usually good potential to improve your USPs for products, services and customer segments. And this starts with picking your first segment, as you did earlier by applying 80/20 analysis. Then, define your USP for this segment.

Ask yourself:

- Is this USP unique and special?
- Does it accurately communicate exactly what you want to sell to your prospects?
- Does it effectively motivate you clients to buy from you as your communication reaches them?
- Are you happy with this USP as a representation of who you are and what you are offering?
- Will this USP generate the sales you want to produce from this segment?

Note that the closer that your USP is matched to your target client, the more unique it will be for those clients, and the greater will be their compulsion to buy your offer.

For more about your USP, read on…

4. Improve your USP

Your USP is comprised of 4 parts, easily remembered from the acronym POPE:

Product or service: The product / service that you package for these clients.

Offer: The offer you make to get them to take action and buy from you.

Promise: The promise you deliver once you have sold to them.

Experience: The experience your client has from buying from you.

Take every opportunity to match your offer as closely as possible to the "problem" your customer wants solving. You may find it useful to think in terms of your customer's reason for buying. What problem are they buying to solve?

Your offer must make them buy, pick up the phone to you, whatever is the next logical step you want them to take. It must be powerful enough to create action from the prospect. It must generate the thought in your prospect's mind, "Yes, I want that".

Think of your promise as being your promise to solve the problem that your customer has bought from you to solve. Do you fully solve that problem? Make sure that your product or service produces the outcome expected by your customer.
The experience is that which you provide to your customer as they buy from you and as you deliver your solution to their problem. Never underrate your buyer's experience.

Think of experience in terms of the old adage:

A person will never remember everything that you have said, but they will always remember how you made them feel.

Design the experience part of your USP to ensure that your customer feels good about buying from you.

Think about luxury goods. When you buy an expensive car or designer handbag, it is not just about solving a simple problem. But it is about how the purchase makes you feel.

Take every opportunity to ensure that your client feels positive about buying from you. And make sure that you define this experience as part of your USP for every product and service that you provide.

5. Fine-tune your USP

It is usually beneficial to fine tune your USP by checking and adjusting the "Ps of your or your offer:

Product (or service): Is your product uniquely matched to the solution wanted by your client? Could you cost effectively adjust it to make it unique for them? Is it possible to produce the required outcome for the client and reduce your product or delivery costs?

Pricing: Is your pricing correct for your client? Is it the optimum for you? Can you use your pricing strategically to further your sales objectives?

Place: Is the place where you do your business matched to your USP? Luxury goods are sold in luxurious and exclusive settings. Make sure that the places your clients see your products are the optimal places to create sales. Make sure that all the media you use to advertise and promote your products is the right media for your target client.

Packaging: If you sell a beautiful solution to your client's problem, do you package it beautifully? Rolex watches come in expensive, beautiful boxes. Make sure that your packaging reflects positively on your product or service. If you sell a brilliant service, make sure that your brochure reflects this. Remember that your job is about your customer feeling good, and your packaging must be designed to manage this.

Position: Your USP may be unique for a particular price point in your overall market. But it may well be possible for you to change your price and product to establish another position that is more profitable or desirable for you. There is more about positioning throughout this book.

Promotion: Look at how you currently promote your products. How do you sell and deliver them? Where do you advertise and how do you stimulate demand? Is there any opportunity to open up new and more effective ways to promote to your prospects?

How many ways do you currently promote your products into your market? Is that enough to create a constant and predictable demand?

Process: What are your processes for selling and delivering your products or service? How to optimise these has been discussed in more detail in other strategy sections. Can you find any opportunities to fine tune these processes and positively influence the POPE of your products?

People: Is everyone in your business trained to put your client first? Are your sales people and delivery people trained well enough to excel in these areas? Is there room for improvement? Could the benefits of training and personal development produce disproportionate improvements in sales revenue?

Explore each of your "Ps" and look for ways to adjust your USP to be as unique as possible. To maximise the differences between your offers and those of your competitors.

6. Look at what your competitors are doing

Always keep an eye on what your competitors are doing in your market. Never be intimidated by their activities. Even though you can see them, you do not know if they are working as intended. Just keep improving what YOU are doing.

The only tactic that always works to set you apart from all your competitors is "get better". This is better in your products and services. Your pricing. Your selling and delivery.

Monitor what your competitors are doing in the light of what you can steal, to open the gap between your products and theirs. Look at what they offer in terms of their USP, their "Ps", their market – media – message congruence and so on. Look for things that you can borrow to add even more value to your offers.

Where you see something that you cannot explain, note it down and return later when you have more knowledge about your customers in that market. Never ever give up your journey to get better. Competitor information is readily available. Use it continually to fine tune your USP.

7. Test and measure your outcomes

When you have a clear focus on what you are doing to improve your outcomes, this produces a clear focus for your testing and measuring. Never test and measure without this focus. Otherwise you suffer a double whammy. One, you waste resources on the T&M. And two, you may get confused by "too much information".

Test and measure every part of your USP to your target clients. Look at your numbers for inputs and outputs. What are your total sales costs? What are your total delivery costs? What margins and profits have these inputs produced?

- Look for qualitative measures. Ask clients what they want more of and less of. Adapt and trial new ways to add to your product – offer – promise – experience. Then ask for feedback from customers.
- Look for and test ways to achieve more repeat buying. To encourage your clients to refer you to their friends and contacts.
- Make your product easy to buy and easy for them to get their value from it.
- Test and measure every cost you pay and every benefit that you provide. This is the only sure way that I know you will establish a continually improving USP with consequent effect upon your sales revenue and profits.
- Look for the opportunity to offer "add on" or next generation products and services. People who buy this, may also want that. For example: If your offer is high priced, there may be a finance element that you can provide.

You'll note how major car manufacturers make it easier for customers to buy with their finance deals. And their finance businesses are usually sound and highly profitable businesses in their own right.

Testing and measuring sets you in the right direction, so stay on this path until you are satisfied that your USP is good enough for now. Then switch your efforts to another product USP and repeat the process.

Sales strategy challenge four:
How to use marketing to improve your profits

Strategy checklist	Doing this!	Do more!	Start doing!
1: Focus your scarce resources			
2: Use 80/20 analysis to find your focus			
3: Revisit your USP			
4: Improve your USP			
5: Fine-tune your USP			
6: Look at your competitors			
7: Test and measure your outcomes			
TOTAL			

Transfer your totals to the table on Page 310

Sales strategy challenge five: How to build more profit by repositioning your products/services

Positioning is often misunderstood. The best definition we have found is from the book *Positioning* by Al Ries and Jack Trout:

> *"Positioning is not what you do to a product.*
> *Positioning is what you do in the mind of the prospect."*

There is a delay between what you do to reposition your products and services, and how your prospects think about them. Hence adjusting positioning must be meticulously planned.

You may find that relatively small changes in your communication strategy yield highly disproportionate results. But if you sense that there are extra profits to be had by improving your positioning, then immediately start analysing and implementing your options.

Repositioning can take time for its effects to show up in profits. But when it does, the effects can be amazing.

Here are 7 things to try and do. Try them out and see if they fit. Then choose the ones that work best for you.

1. Be aware of the importance of positioning

Optimal positioning of your offers is important because:

- You communicate exactly what makes you special to the prospects in your market.
- You stand out so your prospects can find you in a crowded market.
- Your ideal customer can easily recognise and buy what you are offering them.

- Your position shows your prospects how well you understand them and their needs.
- You look like an expert in your target market.

In effect, you are front of their mind when they look to buy what you are offering. You occupy that space in their thinking so that they think of you first when they want to buy.
Even better, when they speak to other people who want to buy your type of products and services, they will recommend you without any hesitation.

2. Write down your customers' '100 problems'

You may think that you "have the best product since sliced bread" but that is irrelevant to increasing your sales. It is what your prospect and buyer thinks that matters when they decide to buy.

Therefore, to reposition you must get into your prospect's mind and out of your own head.

There are various ways to get inside your prospects' heads and one highly valuable way is to write a list of "The 100 problems that my customer has". This sounds initially like a lot of work but we can tell you that this works very successfully. It creates an understanding of your client, their needs, wants and mind-set like nothing else we have every used.

This list will produce a vast amount of messaging material for you to communicate how well you understand your clients. Write down 100 problems and you will always have information to talk to your clients. This information will show them how well you know them and their challenges.

They will know that you are listening to them. Your marketing will contain lots of value and relevance to them. And you will be better able to match your product and service offers to their exact needs.

3. Find out what frustrates your typical buyer in your marketplace

You may feel tempted to try to find out what your prospects think about your product/service offer. However, there will be difficulty and cost associated with this and in fact it is not the best approach to take.

If you have written your "The 100 problems that my customer has" you will see mismatches between your offer and the needs and wants of your clients. This will then help you to redefine your offers to match them more closely to your clients.

Use test and measure as you do this refinement and you will gradually re-position your products, yourself, and your business in the mind of your client.
If you want a quick win, you can just look at what frustrates your buyer when they buy in your market. What is it when they buy that gets on their nerves? Then make sure that you do not do this, and communicating this via your marketing and sales will attract more clients.

You have a clear barometer for this repositioning and that is your sales revenue per product. Make sure you can track this effectively as you make changes in your repositioning.

4. Find your repositioning focus

You cannot reposition every product and service at one time. You will never work with this level of complexity. You must create a focus for repositioning.

So, analyse your sales numbers per product and service. And by type of customer. Use 80/20 analysis to confirm which products, services and customers provide a disproportionate profit in your business.

Check whether you can supply more of these products and services to your customers. And make sure that you have the money and other resources to market, sell and deliver increased quantities of these products and services to your target customers.

Make sure that you can overcome any other barriers and resistance you may meet increasing your sales to these target clients before you start to reposition to them.

Then start your repositioning to these target clients, using test and measure to track increases in sales, costs, and profitability.

5. Find the best ways to improve communication with target customers

Once you have refined what you must communicate to your target customers, you must find the most effective way to communicate this to them. Because your communication is now better matched to their wants, needs and mind-set, it will have more impact. But you must still match your improved message to your media and to your market.

You may simply just turn up the volume of your current marketing and you can easily test and measure the effects of this. But after taking time and effort to discover more about what is going on in the mind of your target customers, why not restructure your message to communicate more quality, value and relevance to them. You are then using your existing media to deliver a more relevant message to your target customers.

But you may also consider exploring media that is more relevant to these target customers. You can then have the benefit of a better message delivered through a better media, and this will reduce your client acquisition cost. Then you will not only sell more to these target customers, you will also improve margin and profit in doing so.

Make sure that you test and measure throughout every repositioning process. This will reduce your wastage, and maximise your returns.

6. Keep repositioning

Understand that repositioning is a journey. Because of the complexity and change within any market you will never arrive at a perfect position. This is because your existing position is continually being undermined by everything that is happening in your market.

You do not have to establish an ideal position - you just need to establish a position that produces enough advantage in your market to generate the level of sales that you can deliver and finance.

If you watch a horse race, the first three places are winners. The winner gets the most prize money and then 2nd and 3rd also win money. But in getting a sale there are no 2nd and 3rd places. If you don't get the 1st place, the sale, you get nothing.

In a horse race the winner can win the race by just a "nose", about 3 inches or so. And for you to win sales all you need is that "nose". You don't have to win by much margin. But you do not want to be pushed into 2nd place and get nothing after you have invested your resources on your prospects.

Effective repositioning will help you win by more than a "nose", and you will quickly see the difference in your sales revenue.

As your positioning is eroded you will see a reduction in sales to those target clients. Once you pick this up from your sales figures, it is time to reposition again. This is the next step in your positioning journey.

7. Monitor your repositioning progress

The closer that your offer matches the needs of your customer, the more they will buy from you. They will remain loyal and they will keep coming back. You will see your repositioning working when you notice:

- Sales in your repositioned segment show a sustainable increase.
- Your marketing and selling processes working more effectively.
- You note reduced selling and buying resistance from customers.
- Your customer relations become easier – transactions are more fluid and occur without any pressure.

In effect, you sell more to your target customers and you sell and deliver your products and services at a reduced cost.

To increase your sales, continue to develop and test new offers until your offers are matched closer and closer to their ideal. Then communicate these improved offers to your chosen segment using your improved knowledge about what is going on in the mind of your target client.

Sales strategy challenge five:
How to build more profit by repositioning your products/services

Strategy checklist	Doing this!	Do more!	Start doing!
1: Be aware of the importance of positioning			
2: Write down customers' '100 problems'			
3: Find out what frustrates your buyer			
4: Find your repositioning focus			
5: Find the best ways to improve communications			
6: Keep repositioning			
7: Monitor your repositioning progress			
TOTAL			

Transfer your totals to the table on Page 310

Sales strategy challenge six:
How to identify and improve your selling mindset

As you work to improve your business results you may have noticed that some things remain beyond your grasp. You want to do them, you need to do them, but you don't. You may rationalise this by saying to yourself and others: "I'll do that later; when I have more time; after my holidays; when I get some more information; after I've done this more important job" and so on.

But the net result is that certain jobs just do not get done as often or as well as they need to be. And it is these jobs which you must identify and then adjust your mind-set to getting them done.

Here are 7 things to try and do. Try them out and see if they fit. Then choose the ones that work best for you.

1. Monitor the things you avoid doing

If the outcomes from your business fall short of your expectations, do not think that you are lacking in some way. Just start to notice and accept that what got you here will not get you there. Einstein said:

*"We cannot solve our **PROBLEMS** with the same **THINKING** we used when we **CREATED** them."*

Begin to identify and note any resistance, habits and behaviours that get in the way of your success. We all have these. And the first step to overcoming them is to become aware. Then we can start making positive changes.

We recommend that you take note of things that you know that you should do but don't.

"I keep not doing things around: ___________"

And then insert the activity in here. This will start to make you more aware of what you are not doing, and what it is costing you. Then when you are ready, you can get a specialist to help you overcome the resistance, and change your habits and behaviours.

2. Work on pricing resistance

The best explanation that we have read about pricing resistance comes from Dan Kennedy in his book *No B. S. Price Strategy*. Paraphrasing from page 90 of that book, he says:

"There are two chains that bind product to price: one is in the customer's mind and the other is in yours. BOTH must be cut. It's a near certainty that the chain in your mind is bigger, thicker, stronger than the one in the customer's mind.

Customers embrace de-linking product and price routinely, given reason to do so. Business owners and salespeople are, ironically more committed to the linkage. In this case, as in most, income improvement will follow self-improvement."

If this resonates with you, at least know where to start to de-link your pricing. The techniques to unravel your thinking are outside the scope of this section but start by buying Dan Kennedy's book. And go straight to page 89 to achieve a great payback on your time.

Do you feel that you underprice and/or oversupply your products and services? If you do, then you are probably right. Stop wasting your time and money, by getting help right now. Look for a coach or a mentor who is suitable qualified to help you with this.

3. Check your selling processes

In **sales strategy two**, we suggested that you write down your selling processes. Go back to these and look at those steps in which you perform worst. Those steps where you feel tension. Where you would like to perform better.

A common step that creates tension is closing. Asking for the order. This triggers all sorts of mind-set chatter and resistance.

Another step is in establishing exactly what is your prospect's problem and matching your solution exactly to that. You may ramble, lose sight of their problem, or generally do a substandard job in identifying your customer's problem and then selling your solution to them.

Look for resistance, habits and behaviours as you perform your selling processes.

And don't forget to do the same in your delivery processes. Just note any resistance, habits and behaviours as

"I keep not doing things around: ____________"

and insert the activity in here.

4. Write down your beliefs in relation to your selling

A nuance in the language of English people is that we use the "softer" word 'reason' instead of the word 'excuse'. Note that every reason is still an excuse even if we describe it differently.

And we all have excuses, even you. Start by writing them down as you make them to yourself, to your customers, your loved ones, your team, and everyone you speak to.

Your excuses are your language and your language creates your reality. If you believe there is a very good reason for you not to do something, guess what, you will not do it.

Therefore, looking through your selling activities, note your reasons, as they are in fact your excuses. They have got you here, they will not get you there.

When you note any resistance, habits and behaviours as

"I keep not doing things around: ____________".

And insert the activity in here.

In the same place, note what reasons you are making for not completing what you know that you should, and within the time you agreed that you would complete it.

Awareness is always the first step to solving any challenge. So, raise your awareness, start today.

5. Face up to your sales excuses

We speak our reasons (which are in fact just excuses) because we cannot easily speak our beliefs. But each of our beliefs can give rise to many reasons why we do not perform as we know that we should.

Check over the following list of beliefs that can affect our selling ability. If you see any that resonate with you, identify and write down the habit or behaviour you feel is most associated with that belief:

- I can't stand up and talk in front of these people – they'll laugh, they'll think I am stupid, I have nothing worthwhile to tell them etc.
- If I increase my prices, my customers will fall out with me and go elsewhere.
- People will think and speak bad of me unless I under-price and/or over-deliver.
- I can't possibly do that – I'm not educated enough / I'm not smart enough / I am not good enough / I don't have the skills
- That kind of success is way beyond my status, ability, knowledge etc. – I'll never achieve that.
- I want people to always think well of me – then I'll be OK.
- I can't let people get to know who I really am – they will not like me.
- Success means far more responsibilities – will I cope? Will there be anyone to help me?
- Success is unpredictable – better to stay safe where I am now

These are just a selection of the beliefs that we have heard, and all of them undermine our ability to sell. I think that selling is where most beliefs and resistance show up, because this is the area where most business owner-managers are pushed furthest out of their comfort zones.

6. Identify and overcome sales resistance

There are many examples of sales resistance that spill out of our meetings with clients. We have yet to develop immunity to some of these! Do you see any that resonate with you? If so, then you know where you can start making improvements:

- Talking too much instead of listening.
- Not following up with clients who say "No".

- Not following up quickly enough with clients who say "Yes".
- Can you tell prospects and customers your price without any hesitation?
- Do you have a reply ready for when you tell them your price and they quiz you on it by saying something like:
  - "That seems a bit high"
  - "I can't afford that"
  - "What do I get for that?"
- Are you authentic and confident when speaking about and promoting your business?
- Do you have a practiced pitch when you meet people and they ask you what you do?
- Are you practiced and know what to say to clients who complain?
- Can you turn their complaint around to strengthen your relationship with them?
- How comfortable are you calling to follow up after quoting your clients?

There are many other examples. Just find and accept what you do well and not so well. There is huge opportunity for you to build your selling system to maximise your strengths and minimise your weaknesses.

This starts with getting to know yourself better. No-one is perfect, and others will accept us warts and all when we are authentic. Start by becoming more aware of who you are. And then learning how to project this authentically and effectively to your customers.

7. Take your next steps to improve your mindset

Know that there is no perfect way to sell your products to prospects. No perfect way to get them to buy more and keep re-buying.

But it is up to each of us to know when we are being authentic. And to remain authentic in the face of change. In this we have the power to stay constant to ourselves and others.

Our customers will sense when we are not being authentic. Remaining authentic and communicating this in all our dealings with clients allows us to resonate with exactly those clients we work best with. When we are authentic, our communication gets through to them. They see and are attracted to us in their mind.

It is within our power to understand and project our own unique and personal brand. "Who we are on our very best day."

In these matters, knowledge is king. Once we know where we are, we know how far we need to journey. And we are 100% sure and confident in the direction we take.

We know anything that does not take us in that direction will never take us there.

Never look at your results and beat yourself up. At the end of each day take time to consider if you have done your best in the circumstances.

Set off in the right direction, and keep getting better at what you do.

Sales strategy challenge six:
How to identify and improve your selling mindset

Strategy checklist	Doing this!	Do more!	Start doing!
1: Monitor the things you avoid doing			
2: Work on pricing resistance			
3: Check your selling processes			
4: Write down your beliefs in relation to your selling			
5: Face up to your sales excuses			
6: Identify and overcome sales resistance			
7: Improve your mindset			
TOTAL			

Transfer your totals to the table on Page 310

Sales strategy challenge seven: How to manage and motivate your selling team

Your selling team is any member of your internal and external teams who impacts your selling process, your prospects and customers. The chain is only as strong as the weakest link, so everything counts. Your job is to look at every link and work to improve any weaknesses.

Here are 7 things to try and do. Try them out and see if they fit. Then choose the ones that work best for you.

1. **Follow the 4 Ds: Decide – Data – Discuss – Do**

Decide how many sales you want and by when. Then drop down into more details about client segments and products and pricing. You cannot change everything at once so you must also decide on which changes you will focus your resources on right now.

Find the **Data** that you need to test and measure the changes that you plan. You will already have the data you have used to decide your focus, thus all you need to do here is to work on the how much and by when into the future.

Discuss your plans with your team members and ensure they understand your objectives. **Why** you are focusing here, **what** you want to achieve, **how** you will do this, **who** is responsible for what, **when** the outcomes are due and **where** you expect the outcomes to come from. Get total clarity about the KPNs you are expecting.

Do what you intend. Get started and check your outcomes.

As the results come in continue to follow these 4 Ds. Always **Discuss** with your team and evaluate the outcomes against your original plan and then make adjustments accordingly.

2. Get numbers into your culture

Take the opportunity of using the 4 Ds to bring numbers into your culture. Make quantitative measures a part of "how you do things here".

To reduce discussion and opinions in your team meetings, teach and encourage your team members to individually report their results as numbers. If the numbers do not measure the inputs and outcomes that you want, encourage your team to find new numbers that are more representative of the facts.

When you operate with the correct KPNs, you will find it much easier to steer your business. Because each individual has clarity on what is expected from them, the process runs more smoothly and efficiently. The team is cohesive, they have a clear focus, everything is simpler, and this creates a sustainable and increasing momentum.

And most importantly your job of co-ordinating the efforts of your team becomes much easier, leaving you more time to focus on the next area of your business that requires your attention.

Of course, do not forget that you may need some qualitative measures. If you don't manage to define these at the outset, you may find and include them during the 4 Ds process.

3. Ensure nothing happens until somebody sells something

Remember this process is about outcomes. And the main outcome is increasing your sales in your chosen market segment via a managed, logical and consistent process.

You will know your process is working when sales start to increase. Up until that point everything is just extra inputs with nothing concrete to show. Keep your attention on your sales. When the increase comes, push it as far as you can. If the increase does not come, dig and dig until you find exactly what you must change to generate an improvement.

This is an iterative process, keep testing changes and measuring outcomes. Check the numbers - daily, weekly and monthly, throughout the selling process + the delivery process.

But always keep in mind "nothing happens until somebody sells something."

4. Remove every reason why you don't sell more

As you Decide – Data – Discuss – Do, you will discover reasons why your selling process and the individuals operating it do not sell more. Take note of all these reasons, as these provide direction and focus for your main input to this change process. And this is to take away all the reasons one by one.

Because, as you take away each reason, you make each member of your team more accountable. Initially they can tell you, "It's not me – it's this reason". Once you remove their reasons, they must accept it is their responsibility and get on and produce the expected outcomes.

The reasons may be connected to personal motivation and solutions to these lie in using your management and leadership skills to unearth and solve them. But do check that your sales tools provide maximum support to your sales efforts. Discuss with your team exactly what they require in terms of support materials: Sales presentations; brochures; flyers; product information; price list and pricing explanations; selling scripts for presenting and follow-up etc.

Check everything that they currently use to make their sales. Make sure it is the very best that you can afford right now. High quality and effective sales materials improve the performance of every sales person. Even when they are a natural at selling. Sales materials are a very cost effective way to improve the performance of those people who are not natural sales people. Remember – everything counts.

5. Keep improving your selling and delivery processes

At your team meetings, take time to review each of your selling and delivery processes. Look for and discuss how you can improve any friction points in these processes. Ask for suggestions how these can be eased or speeded up.

Review your sales tools and discuss the effectiveness of these for every user. Note that what works well for one person can feel awkward or clunky for another. Supply each individual with the best tools for them to sell and deliver.

Take time to discuss additional or more specific training for your team members. Does everyone perform at their best in these processes? It's your job to keep finding and asking the questions. Then ensure every individual in your team does their very best to make the improvements.

Look for and discuss any ways you can cost-effectively sell and deliver more value to your clients' purchases. Calculate the additional profit this would generate for your business. Is this worth the effort?

Brainstorm how you can improve processes and systems to reduce costs and increase profits. Encourage creativity and new ideas. There are no bad suggestions, no-one is allowed to ridicule any idea. Every idea is valuable, because you never know where it will lead.

Everyone must be included. You never know where the next good idea will come from. Lead and train your team to come up with ideas and suggestions and you will never look back. And don't forget to reward individuals for their ideas and suggestions.

6. Set individual and team targets

To maximise creativity, create focus. This stops you scattering your creativity and other resources.

Use targets and milestones to provide focus and keep all your efforts on track. You are either hitting these or not; you are on your way to them or not. They provide clarity for your efforts and communication.

To drive your sales, always set ambitious targets in the selling area, both individually and as a sales group. By creating a focus on producing sales, this drags everyone else in the business into servicing sales.

Take care to set the right targets and measure the right things to ensure your success. Be clear about both the inputs and outputs required from each team and individual, and hold everyone (even you) accountable for these.

But do not allow the culture of hitting targets, no matter what, to take hold. You must maintain cohesion in your team. Always have the targets in mind, but encourage your team to support each other 100% of the time. Remember the definition of Team:
Together, **E**veryone **A**chieves **M**ore.

Don't forget to celebrate both team and individual successes. Never leave yourself out of these celebrations - you are the conductor of your orchestra, so be prepared to take your bow.

Focus on your internal team but don't forget your external team. If you don't ask, the answer is definitely "No". Make sure that you ask anyone and everyone who can help you reach your objectives.

7. Create a sales culture in your business

Remember that culture (the way we do things here) is 100% your responsibility. Making sure that sales are a big part of your culture will focus everyone's attention on sales.

Make sure that sales are always talked about. The positives and negatives about your sales should always be on the agenda. Keep sales centre stage.

Keep customers at the centre of discussions within your team. Be clear about what your customers want and expect from you.

Simon Philips discusses the **7 Pillars of Success.** These are:

1) **Focus:** Keep your team as tightly focused as possible. Use quantitative and qualitative data to maintain this focus.
2) **Simplicity:** Keep everything as simple as possible. Just enough information and no more. Just enough to create the results you require and no more.

3) **Cohesion:** Take every step to maintain cohesion within your internal and external teams. Cohesive teams always perform better. Make sure that all incentive and reward systems pass the "cohesion test."
4) **Pace:** Get the first three and things speed up.
5) **Conviction:** Make sure that everyone believes that they can achieve their goals and milestones. If they don't believe – they can't do.
6) **Enterprise:** Create a spirit of enterprise in your business. Encourage everyone to discuss their ideas freely and let them experiment with customers and the market. Be open to letting people pursue some of their own ideas. Never stifle creativity – allow it to flourish.
7) **Greatness:** You cannot be the best in the whole world, but you can be the best in your world. Put your clients at the very centre of what you do, and they will show you how great they think you are by buying from you, again and again.

For over 20 years we have found these useful to explain the fundamentals of any business. And as a quick checklist when we encounter other businesses as potential customers or suppliers. We hope that you find them useful.

Sales strategy challenge seven:
How to manage and motivate your selling team

Strategy checklist	Doing this!	Do more!	Start doing!
1: Follow the 4 Ds: Decide – Data – Discuss - Do			
2: Get numbers into your culture			
3: Ensure nothing happens until someone sells something			
4: Remove every reason why you don't sell more			
5: Keep improving your processes			
6: Set individual and team targets			
7: Create a sales culture in your business			
TOTAL			

Transfer your totals to the table on Page 310

Part 4

Delivery strategy Seven x7

Seven common challenges in delivery strategy

<u>Delivery strategy Seven x7</u>

<u>Seven common challenges in delivery strategy</u>

Now that we have looked at personal, business and sales strategies, it's time to deliver! This creates a whole new set of challenges, which we look at via seven key issues, all with 7 action points. As in the other sections, these action points are then used to create a checklist at the end of each section, so that you can see what progress you are making with each one.

Delivery strategy challenge one: I want a bigger business – What do I need to consider?

"If your business does not grow – it will die." So goes the quote.

Certainly, your lifestyle depends upon your business and you may as well grow it while the market allows you to. In any market, you have a certain window of opportunity to start and grow a business before the window starts to close and the opportunity is lost.

Taking maximum advantage of your window of opportunity right now allows you to make more money and then spend some of this in areas such as building your team, sales and marketing etc. to give you a more predictable and secure foothold in your market.

Here are 7 things to think and do. Try them out and see if they fit. Then choose the ones that work best for you.

1. **Decide why you want a bigger business**

Ask yourself, "What will this give me that I don't have right now?" Don't just let your thoughts go round and round in your head. Capture your thoughts and get clarity by writing them down or drawing pictures. Make sure that you know why you want a bigger business.

Earlier in this book, we encouraged you to think about and write down your current status in seven x7 areas of your personal and business strategy. These should have helped you to clarify where you are now and where you want to get to.

If, once you have evaluated that, you feel emboldened to develop a bigger business, then great! Be clear why it is you have reached that decision and then let's see how the next 6 points can help to reinforce your decision.

2. **Work out why you don't already have a bigger business**

There may be a lack of skills, strategies, knowledge. Just think these over and write down these barriers. You may sense other resistances or fears. Note this also. Doing this starts to focus your mind on looking for options to overcome all obstacles.

It's very common to find that once you focus on something you need, that you will encounter the person, book, article or information that solves that obstacle or allows you to make progress with it. It is unlikely for this to happen until you have brought the obstacle to mind.

Do not judge yourself here, but understand that "What got you here will not get you there". Think of BE – DO – HAVE. You need to BE that person who can DO those things that must be done to HAVE what you want.

You will find that becoming aware of your challenges sets you well on the road to finding their solutions.

3. **Deliver your very own personal brand**

It's no accident that the biggest brands in the world are the most valuable, because they earn so much for their owners. But branding is not just for big companies. You can build your very own brand by being authentic within your market.

You will get known as the go-to person for certain products or services. You can start to travel the branding route and grow your business by consistently communicating to your market. Why you do what you do. What you do. And how you do it. Gradually you will become known for your personal brand.

Your authenticity will attract more of the customers that suit your brand. This happens because your potential clients can see who you are and then be confident to decide whether they will engage with you or not.

Start by writing your story about you and your business. Why you do what you do? What you do, and how you do it? And then tell it to everyone you meet. And as your story develops, watch your business grow.

4. **Deliver your product and service promises with actions not just words**

By all means say what you will deliver to your clients, as this will get you sales. But know that as you deliver, they will be watching everything that you do.

The human fight or flight response is tuned in to look for authenticity. It's impossible to hide who we are for very long. And where customers cannot read our authenticity, they err on the side of caution and buy elsewhere.

You cannot be liked by everyone you meet – that's unrealistic. But being authentic with everyone you meet opens the door for them to decide whether you are a threat or an opportunity, friend or foe.

They will not want to waste their time and energy chasing people they do not see as an opportunity and neither should you.

Your authenticity is your personal brand. It's who you show up as on your very best day. Create solid, automatic habits for when you meet and interact with others. These actions create and project your personal brand. Think Dale Carnegie: "How to Win Friends and Influence People". But do this authentically. Always be yourself, and watch your business grow.

5. **Use the 80/20 rule to focus your business activities**

The 80/20 rule says that 20% of resources will produce 80% of your results. Your task, if you choose to accept it, is for you to find your 20% and then focus as much of your time as possible on those activities.

If you work alone without any help, these high return jobs may take up more than 20% of your time. But some jobs will still produce disproportionate results and it is these that you must focus on.

Start by listing all the jobs that ONLY you can do. And then list all the others that you do. This gets your mind working on which jobs you should pay someone else to do. As you delegate to others, focus your freed-up time on doing more of those jobs that only you can do.

Typical examples of work that only business owners can do in their business: Selling; marketing; finding customer prospects; building and managing internal and external teams; negotiating with suppliers etc.

Typical examples of work that others could do: Bookkeeping; administrative jobs; managing your diary; after sales follow-up; collecting money; paying bills; telesales prospecting; research etc.

Start delegating now!

6. **Employ the right people to help you to grow your business**

Consider, if you could double the amount of time you spent on your 20% of high return jobs. Then calculate how much you could afford in order to buy the help that allows you to do this.

The 80% jobs list creates the job specification for your helper. From this you will know what a helper is worth to you and what you want them to take from you. So, get started looking for that person

Take note that this works as you build your internal team of direct employees. And your external team – suppliers, consultants, specialist service providers such as business advisors, branding and marketing consultants, web and social media service providers etc.

The clarity you get from applying the 80/20 rule will help you when measuring the effectiveness of anyone you employ. Keep using it as you grow your business.

7. **Use your culture to grow your business**

Definition of Culture: "The way we do things here."

Becoming ever more consistent in the way you do things will help you to grow your business. There are no successful businesses that have an inconsistent or weak culture.

The only way to grow your business is to enlist others to help. You cannot do it alone. And to do this you must have clarity and openness in the way that you manage all activities with both your internal and external teams.

Remember that we are all tuned into looking for inconsistency and making instant judgments about each other. Therefore, you create a strong culture by being authentic and consistent in the language that you use and the ways in which you do what you say:

- By how you make your expectations clear when dealing with others.
- By what you do when your expectations are not met as you intended.
- And by how you deal with individuals when you have not met their expectations.

Start by examining every individual relationship that you have in your business. Do these work exactly as you would wish? Pick the ones that you want to work better and focus on improving these by adjusting your language and actions.

Here are some questions you may need to confront and answer if a situation arises that requires you to fix an individual relationship:

- When did I notice this?
- Who is involved?
- What exactly have they done?
- What feelings has this set off in me?
- How (and why) did I let them do that?
- What will I do to stop them now?
- How can I achieve this with them?
- What will I do to avoid this recurring in future?

We have found that the Four Agreements by Don Miguel Ruiz is invaluable to understanding and achieving more productive and enjoyable relationships:

- Be impeccable with your word
- Don't take anything personally
- Don't make assumptions
- Always do your best

Delivery strategy challenge one:
I want a bigger business – What do I need to consider?

Delivery checklist	Doing this!	Do more!	Start doing!
1: Decide why you want a bigger business			
2: Work out why you don't already have a bigger business			
3: Deliver your very own personal brand			
4: Deliver your promises with actions			
5: Use the 80/20 rule to focus			
6: Employ the right people			
7: Use your culture to grow your business			
TOTAL			

Transfer your totals to the table on Page 311

Delivery strategy challenge two: How can I do less work and make more money?

This is probably the No 1 question for most business owners. It's also encapsulated in the well know phrase, "Work Smarter, Not Harder". We all talk about this. But how can we achieve it?

Here are 7 things to think and do. Try them out and see if they fit. Then choose the ones that work best for you.

1. Increase your hourly rate

To calculate your approximate hourly rate, just take your monthly salary and divide this by the number of hours you work per month.

£4,000 per month divided by 160 hours (40 per week) is £25/hour.

To do less work and make more money you must increase the amount of money that you can earn per hour. If you can double your hourly rate, you can either reduce your working hours by 20 hours per week, or use these 20 hours to earn more.

You achieve this is by focusing on those jobs that produce the biggest disproportionate return on your time. You apply the 20/80 principle. If you are fortunate, then these 20% are the jobs that you love, and are likely to be ultra-productive for you.

Often the 20% are jobs that only you can do. Many sales jobs such as presenting and closing sales are very high hourly rates. Often in the £000s per hour.

Many jobs in the remaining 80% will be jobs that are not productive use of your time, that you are probably not skilled at and are not productive for you. Delegate these to others to free up time that you can use more productively.

Find and reduce all low hourly rate jobs that you work. Pay someone else to do jobs such as bookkeeping, general administration work, booking your appointments etc.

2. Test and measure – with focus

Someone once asked us what is the number one thing that always works in business. We told them it is testing and measuring.

But T&M costs resources, so you must focus your T&M efforts. You do this by looking for your main business challenges and focusing there. If you need more sales, then focus your T&M on your sales and marketing activities and processes.

If you need to cut costs and increase margins, focus your T&M on your delivery processes and systems. Once you decide where to focus, you must find the choke points that limit overall efficiencies and then decide the KPNs to test and measure.

Study processes and systems - study what people do and how they do it: Staff, suppliers and customers

Keep these three things in mind:

- What you can measure, you can manage.
- Einstein said: "Not everything that can be counted counts, and not everything that counts can be counted."
- Don't focus only on quantitative measures. It is also possible to create measures for most qualitative parts of most businesses. Think McDonald's, who measure everything, including how the staff dress and how they greet and connect with you.

3. Work to deliver the highest value promise at your best cost to the most clients

Business is about being paid to deliver a value promise to the customer. The difference between your cost to deliver this promise and the price paid by the customer is the profit.

Note that our clients are usually not as price conscious as we believe them to be. But we can always assume they are value conscious. Before deciding to buy, they intuitively look at the value we offer and unconsciously compare this to their inner map. To make more money and do less, you can mix and match four main options:

- Sell the same value more cheaply by lowering your cost of acquiring clients and delivering your value.
- Sell more of the same value promises to the same clients.
- Sell more of the same value promises to different clients.
- Increase your prices and sell the same number of value promises.

Of course, you can apply test and measure first to establish the workability of these options. Do not expand your sales without considering how to expand delivery to match increased sales. Otherwise you may sacrifice customer satisfaction.

4. Improve your delivery methods to reduce costs and improve profits

Create focus before diving in and measuring everything. The best place to start is to write down your delivery processes. Use one sheet of paper for each process, writing only one or two lines per step.

Then estimate and add your costs to each step. This produces an overview of the delivery process and where money is spent to satisfy clients. Start from the delivery step where you spend the most money and then work through the rest.
This will help to answer questions such as:

- Are you getting paid the right amount for your effort?
- Which activities are costing you the most money?
- Are your clients appreciating the value in each of the steps?
- Are you and your clients BOTH getting value for money from these costly steps?
- Without decreasing the OVERALL value to your clients, can you see any ways to reduce costs?

Make sure that you are not adding cost to give your clients something that they do not perceive as valuable.

You'll get paid more for doing less by using test and measure to produce the optimum match between your delivery cost and the value perceived by your clients.

As a bonus, you may also find other ways to improve your profit per sale by selling higher perceived value offers at higher prices and disproportionate cost to your business.

5. Improve your selling processes to reduce costs and improve profits

There can be some quick wins from increasing the efficiency of your sales processes in order to reduce the cost of acquiring new customers. But you need to create focus before diving in and measuring everything.

To make this more manageable, segment your market by type of product, type of client, price point of offer etc. Use one sheet of paper for each sales segment and write one or two lines for each step of the sales process. Then estimate and add your costs to each step.

This produces an overview of the sales process and identifies where money is spent to acquire clients. Start from the sales step where you spend the most money and then work through the rest.

This will help to answer questions such as:

- Overall what is your cost to acquire each customer?
- Which activities in each sales process are costing you the most money?
- Is there opportunity to increase the efficiency of each activity?

Without decreasing the OVERALL efficiency of each sales process, can you see any ways to adjust the costly steps to reduce costs, without decreasing your conversion rate?

Remember that the major factor in sales performance is not the person – it is the tools and the process. Sales tools such as brochures, factsheets, scripts, etc. are cheap ways to gain faster and cheaper sales conversions.

For more quick wins, use test and measure to investigate the processes you use to get repeat sales from existing clients.

For more detail about increasing efficiency in the selling area, see the Sales strategy seven x7.

6. Add value through the delivery and sales processes, and increase prices

Most businesses achieve quick wins by simple testing and measuring of their delivery and sales processes. This quickly increases profit that could be spent to grow more profit.
Usually it is possible to find ways to add extra perceived value to your offers and products. And selling this at higher prices to increase sales margin.

There are many customers who want "the best they can afford". And there is often the opportunity to bolt on more value and charge a disproportionately higher price for this. Every day you will see many real-world examples of "premium products" or services.

There can be ways to create and price value during the sales process. For example, it is common in some business sectors to discuss a client's needs and then compile a proposal of some sort that is then sent to the client. To create this proposal often requires significant investment in resources. Hopefully this is paid for by those clients who eventually buy.

These proposals often represent value to clients. They may use them as internal or external discussion documents. Even to help in searches for alternative suppliers. Packaging and selling the value in these proposals to clients can provide sales revenue.

For some quick wins, become more aware of exactly how you sell and deliver your products and services. And start looking for ways to achieve more for less.

7. Use technology and IT to improve productivity

Enlist the right help when this is not your area of expertise. It is relatively cheap to get a technology survey done for all your delivery and other processes. You may even be able to get this for no upfront cost.
Create a focus by surveying not only how you deliver your products and services, but also how you sell and get paid for them. The more work that you do to improve focus, the easier will be the job for your technology expert.

Remember it is their job to match a technology solution to the needs of your business. Don't assume that they will understand the needs of your business. It is your job to focus his or her attention to those areas where you get the fastest, biggest return on investment

Plan well and do well. As in all major spending projects – do your homework. Or have someone else help you with it.

A few points to consider:

- Work with your technologist to produce a step by step plan for improving your technology and IT.
- Avoid throwing out the old until you've got the new up to speed.
- Expect your technologist to help you to buy from the right suppliers, at the right price.
- Get assurances and guarantees directly from your hardware and software suppliers.
- If you can afford it – retain your technologist to help you get the very best return from your new installation.
- Make sure that you know the costs of and budget for extra training for you and your team during and after the installation.

Delivery strategy challenge two:
How can I do less work and make more money?

Delivery checklist	Doing this!	Do more!	Start doing!
1: Increase your hourly rate			
2: Test and measure – with focus			
3: Deliver highest value at best cost to most customers			
4: Improve delivery to reduce costs and raise profits			
5: Improve selling processes to reduce costs and raise profits			
6: Add value through delivery and sales processes			
7: Use IT to improve productivity			
TOTAL			

Transfer your totals to the table on Page 311

Delivery strategy challenge three:
How do I get my internal team to perform better?

Be clear on who is your team.

Essentially you have three teams, all of which impact your business and your life:

i. **Your Personal Team**: You / your personal support team – Spouse – Family – Friends. Other owners / Directors in your business / Coaches and mentors. All your personal and business contacts
ii. **Your internal team**: Your staff who work only and directly for your business
iii. **Your External Team**: Suppliers; Any other Stakeholders – Banks / Lenders / Investors; And don't forget - Your clients.

Delivery strategy three is about internal team performance. Just imagine that you work your socks off the week before you go on holiday to get things straight. So that there are no surprises for your staff. Everyone knows what they need to do while you are away, and off you go.

Do you ever get back and everything agreed by your internal team has been completed to your satisfaction? Probably not – but what if your team could do this for you?

Here are 7 things to think and do. Try them out and see if they fit. Then choose the ones that work best for you.

1. Decide what a good team should do for you

Firstly, get clarity on what you expect. What needs to change first and why. Usually it's better to back up your gut feel with facts. And you'll get these from your KPNs.

The focus for change and first steps may be in any area, for example:

- Improving your delivery process
- Satisfying more clients
- Increasing sales
- Increasing profits
- Entering a new market
- A new marketing project
- Buying new equipment
- Improving customer service

Just find your first focus for action. Then discuss team development at your next team meeting. Have a clear agenda of what you want to change and why. Then agree the priorities. To keep the meeting focused and to get each and every contribution from your team, let the discussion run wherever it goes, but keep bringing the meeting back onto your agenda.

The job of your team is to solve problems in your business and not leave everything to you. Listen well and you'll note which team members are on-side with you and which are not.

Note, then delegate and share out the actions from this team meeting throughout as many members of your team as possible. This starts the process of you stepping back to lead your team and them stepping up to run your business for you.

Business is a team game. It's your job to lead and manage your team and it's your team's job to manage the business.

2. Work out how to measure the productivity of your team

Focus on your first business challenge: Find the quantitative and qualitative measures that you require to monitor and manage improvements.

Remember Einstein: *"Not everything that can be counted counts, and not everything that counts can be counted."*

General measures such as profitability will not do. You can't manage what you can't measure. To manage improvement, you must find the KPNs that connect team productivity with individual productivity.

Start only with your first business challenge and set the scene at your team meetings. Get their buy-in when deciding the quantitative and qualitative measures that you will monitor.

Examples of quantitative measures:

- Number of orders process by hour/day/week etc.
- Number of hours billed per hour/day/week
- Sales revenue today/week/month etc.

Qualitative measures can prove the most important. For example, measuring customer satisfaction. Devise a short list of questions to ask your customers. What has been good about the service just given? Could you tell us one way that we could improve our service next time we serve you? etc.

Other examples of qualitative measures:

- Ask your team to log your customer comments – both positive and negative.

- Note when any of your team (including yourself) goes that extra mile for a client
- Log day-to-day problems that arise and how your team deals with these.

Report true and fair results at your team meetings and you'll find your team will become creative at producing the results you measure.

3. Start with a change of culture to gain improvements

Your business culture is: *"How we do things around here."*

Your culture is your vision, your plan, and you instil it through your language, actions and leadership. It is 100% your responsibility to set and manage your culture. The strength of culture relates directly to business success.

Your team will not do as you say – they will do as you do, as you let them do. Walk the talk. What you say is important but it's what you consistently do that people will copy.

Creating a strong culture is about being clear about your expectations. Use a "Rules of the game" approach where you list how you expect people to behave. This becomes: Terms and conditions for team members.

Demonstrate how they are measuring up to expectations. Both quantitatively and qualitatively. Take every opportunity every day to guide their behaviour.

Effective delegation and communication reinforce culture. Get good at these skills. Make sure your communication is received as intended. Where you do not get the result you want from any team member, it may be that your communication is not getting through. So, check with them and adapt your message until they can summarise what they need to do and why.

Use rewards and penalties to strengthen culture. Reward and praise a good performance and take poor performers to task immediately. Never think that the rest of your team do not notice an individual poor performer. Highlight which teams and individuals are not performing. Discuss and listen to their reasons and suggestions. Then implement all agreed actions consistently and effectively.

Be patient with culture – the ship may take some time to turn around. But it will eventually go full steam ahead and you will rejoice.

4. Get everyone on the bus – 100% inclusion

Your job is to get everyone 100% committed to being on the bus. Or replace them. Do this as quickly as possible. Every delay costs you time, money and resources.

Adopt your "Rules of the game" approach as Terms and conditions for team members. Set the standards and then act and talk consistently with these standards.

Be prepared for some individuals to say one thing and do another, rather than being open with you. Deal with this fairly and effectively as and when the truth shows up in their results.

Be fair - treat everyone as your employee first and your friend second.

Your leadership is in your language and you may need to make changes.

For example: You may use statements such as "Please do this, do that" etc. However, these are closed and will not usually get good connection and inclusion. So, instead, include them and get their buy-in by asking questions such as:

- "How do you see the problem/challenge/opportunity?"
- "What do you think we/you can/ought to do about that?"

Patiently listen and await their comments without interruption. Give guidance and ask open questions until you both arrive at exactly what needs doing. Then, give them your permission to do it. And thank them for solving the challenge. And don't forget another "thank you for a job well done." Remember that everyone flourishes under praise

Avoid frequent checking with individuals on how they are doing. Get them to report their progress. This builds real strength in your team, enabling you to delegate increasing amounts of work to your team.

5. Improve participation and co-operation within your team

People like to feel that they have done well, and when they have, let them know. Don't hold back. When you get some wins, celebrate these with everyone involved.

Encourage participation and co-operation. Your strong leadership will set the standards you want. Keep the pressure on until your business is proceeding as you want. You must apply firm but gentle pressure every day. And you must be able to measure the effects of any improvements.

Here are some more suggestions to improve participation and co-operation:

- Every meeting, with team and individuals must have an agenda. Otherwise it's just a chat. Also, there must be a result, something to implement, to do, or follow up later. To improve attitude and behaviour talk in terms of your customers. Ask questions such as "If you were our customer what would you want/see/think about us?"
- Write down your Rules of the Game and Terms and conditions for team members in terms of how you want to be seen by your customers.
- Make these rules highly visible and refer to them during meetings when you spot infringements. You are the referee and don't hold back from blowing the whistle.
- Create your expectation of full participation and co-operation.
- Set deadlines - these drive people to co-operate as each deadline approaches.
- When the meeting falls into silence, allow your team some thinking time. Resist the temptation to talk. Instead, let the silence speak and wait for someone else to fill it with an idea or suggestion.

Your business is paying you and your team to solve the challenges. Getting the maximum return depends upon having everyone contributing their ideas openly and fully, keeping the communication flowing, and then implementing as many agreed actions as possible.

6. Implement recruitment policies and procedures

To make it much easier to find the person that you want, make it a rule that you will never start any recruitment process until you have written down exactly what you want them to achieve in your business.

If you are unfamiliar with the current job market and HR legislation, salaries and recruitment processes, then get help. Many people use fixed fee recruitment services which will economically provide exactly the help you need.

There is a recruitment maxim, "Hire slow and fire fast". Do take the time and effort to recruit those people most suited to your culture. Never settle for second best.

If you get it wrong don't waste more by trying to change the attitude of the employee. Just accept you've made a mistake and let them go.

Once you employ the right person, it is crucial that they start to contribute to your business as soon as possible. Prepare the candidate to hit the ground running by being clear about what you want them to do from day 1.

A training plan will help. Typically, this may outline:

- The induction process for the new employee.
- A talk where you or other key staff member ensure that they begin with some understanding of your culture, rules and procedures.
- An outline of their tasks, roles and responsibilities, who they report to etc.
- Who is responsible for their training and development?

- A step-by-step process covering how they will be trained up to full competency.
- Then maybe an outline of what is for them beyond full competency.
- The standard of work required at full competency.
- How their performance will be evaluated.
- What happens if their performance is not up the standard required.
- You will probably include a review period – often three months into the job.

The more clarity you have in these areas, the greater the probability your new recruit will turn out right.

7. Watch for typical team problems and manage them

Typical problems to watch out for are:

- Absence of trust
- Fear of conflict
- Lack of commitment
- Avoidance of accountability
- Inattention to results

You may already see the beginnings of these. If so, it is your job to stop them undermining your progress.

For a strong culture, people must trust that they will be treated fairly and equally. Each employee must trust that their team will help them and that they are expected to help others.

This trust is enhanced when everyone feels comfortable in challenging decisions and performance. You know you have a team built around trust when they can argue with each other without taking it personally and knowing that everyone is focused on the best outcome for the company.

Individual and team underperformance erodes trust. This is common between business owners and key employees. And between individuals pursuing different agendas. It is your job to manage the agenda without being seen to be soft on anyone.

Test and measure quickly reveals any lack of commitment. Employees create many reasons why they don't deliver what they say. Your job is to remove these reasons one by one until they improve their commitment or they move on.

To be successful, never avoid accountability. It is your job to set and maintain standards. Then evaluate everyone (including you) against these standards. And take whatever action is required.

Everyone must pay attention to the results of the business. Resist any temptation to report only the good news and ignore anything that is negative. Ensure that you and your team focus on the true results and deal with them. Quantitative information in KPNs have no opinions and tell no lies.

Delivery strategy challenge three: How do I get my internal team to perform better?

Delivery checklist	Doing this!	Do more!	Start doing!
1: Decide what a good team should do for you			
2: Work out how to measure team productivity			
3: Start with a change of culture			
4: Get everyone on the bus			
5: Improve participation and cooperation			
6: Implement recruitment policies and procedures			
7: Watch and manage team problems			
TOTAL			

Transfer your totals to the table on Page 311

Delivery strategy challenge four: How can I get my external team to perform better?

We all buy services and supplies to improve our businesses: Accountants, lawyers, business advisors and specialists. Most of us have a web site, a graphic designer, a printer and so on. We often buy in services such as telesales, administration support, bookkeeping and payroll etc.

Think about each one of your suppliers. Do you get the best return on your investment from each of them?

Here are 7 things to think and do. Try them out and see if they fit. Then choose the ones that work best for you.

1. **Be clear about what outcomes you want from your external team**

Ensure that both you and any service partner are clear about who is doing what, when, how, why, and where. Start with written objectives and expected outcomes.

Good suppliers will help with this, but they cannot contribute your deep knowledge of the business.

Your initial meetings with them will reveal how they analyse your challenge and how exactly they will help.

Be clear about the expertise you are buying. Exactly what your supplier is providing. And what you as the customer are expected to contribute to make the outcome certain.

Note that many relations break down because the contributors did not do what was expected of them. This is often because the deal was not done with enough clarity in the first place.

Resist any temptation to buy cheap. If your project is worth doing and it generates the right return for you, be prepared to pay the market rate. Negotiate (toughly) at the start, agree the cost and then stick to the agreement. Never try to chisel away once agreed.

Any project is an investment for you. At the outset, write down your expected return. Then review your investment and returns throughout each project.

When necessary, use this information to review and re-negotiate with your supplier.

2. **Get your internal focus clear before you enrol an external team**

Your plan is to buy skills, knowledge and tactics that you do not have internally. Never sit down with any supplier or external team without an agenda. Because without an agenda your meeting is just a chat. To write your agenda when meeting any supplier, take time to define the gap between what you know internally and exactly what you need for your business.

Evaluating potential suppliers is then made easier by you being totally clear about this gap. Because you will be able to start asking the right questions before you've even met them

In your business, you will understand that one of your major challenges is knowing what your customers want from you. You therefore need to get the best from your suppliers by helping them to help you. Do your internal homework first, and have a clear agenda.

Good suppliers will help you gain even greater clarity. But know that your expectations always have the greatest impact on the outcomes.

3. Test and measure to maximise your return on investment (ROI)

Make a point of highlighting in your initial discussions with any supplier, the ROI that you expect from your work together. And then explain how you will test and measure your ROI. Agree what they will do if they do not manage this return for you.

You will rapidly build productive relationships by being open about how you expect suppliers to work with you, and by encouraging them to be open about their expectations from you.

Authenticity, clarity and directness will attract suppliers who are like minded. You do not have the time to waste in unproductive chats with potential suppliers who may have drawn you into their sales agendas.

Frequently we meet and greet potential suppliers. When we are clear what we are looking for, we are much more likely to meet those suppliers who can serve us best.

Thin the herd by asking them right off to guarantee your ROI from employing them. And mention how you will test and measure to hold them to this.

The best suppliers not only guarantee their work but also have clear rules and boundaries that cover expectations from their customers. When your rules and boundaries match theirs, you have got a good match from the start.

Remember that your culture can be defined as "the way we do things here". Never enrol any suppliers who do not match your culture.

4. **Make each supplier in your external team a profit centre**

When you buy any product or service from any supplier, you are buying an investment. Be sure of the return that you expect. Otherwise you are likely to end up disappointed and in dispute.

And we have enough stress and hassle in business without attracting more by having to reset and renegotiate deals with our suppliers.

Recognise and accept that every payment that you make to any supplier must provide an acceptable return for you. You are not buying resources; you are buying results. So, set up quantitative and qualitative measures to track your investment in every supplier.

I guarantee that doing this will almost certainly produce better returns.

Formulate this system on a "How much and by when?" basis. You pay out money and use other resources, and you expect to get back – exactly what and by when?

Tracking the numbers with suppliers in this way will also save you lots of time, money and energy that you will waste if you end up in dispute. Never get embroiled in the "He said - She said" of supplier relationships. Stay focused on the outcomes.

When you can't use numbers, then write and agree specific milestones covering your expected outcomes. Make these as SMART as you can: Specific, Measurable, Achievable, Realistic and Time-bounded.

5. Lead your external team of suppliers

Suppliers who will guarantee you a return on your investment are rare. But even with these, you may find that your leadership will make the difference between an acceptable return and an exceptional return.

It's your job to lead every supplier relationship. Never give up your leadership to any supplier. Set up every external project in a way that allows you to see what is happening. You are paying, so insist on this.

You do not need *War and Peace*, just a simple one or two-page document that covers the main points about the project.

- Who will do what and by when?
- Who needs to receive what from who and by when?

This will prove invaluable:

- As you review each project with each supplier
- As you look for and locate hold ups and bottlenecks
- When you need to make the project go faster

Never assume that everything is on track and going according to plan. And never let project review dates pass without comment. The project is on track, late, or in advance. Communicate this in writing so that individuals know their responsibility to make corrections.

Occasionally a supplier will not produce the expected result and the relationship will need to terminate. Make this clean and clear. Agree who will do what. Who will pay what etc.

You've made an investment, and you've learned some stuff. Don't take it personally. Everyone makes decisions that don't turn out as expected. Then armed with what you've learned, go looking for the next supplier with even more clarity and knowledge.

6. Buy the best suppliers that you can afford

The two key words here are "best" and "afford".

You will get a sense of "best" from the quality of the internal work you do to establish your expectations before you start to talk to suppliers. Your internal work you will also help you to establish a good sense of what you can "afford".

Some questions to help you to structure your thoughts:

- How much will you continue to waste if you do not do the project?
- What is the outcome worth to your business?
- If you achieved this outcome or better, what would you be prepared to pay the supplier who produces this for you?
- How much could you pay to get the outcome you want?

When we do not consider such questions, it is easy to become drawn onto any supplier's sales agenda, and then we end up buying what they want to sell us rather than what we need.

But when we get clear on the downsides and upsides of any our supplier relationship we have a good sense of not only how to evaluate their "best" but also how much we can "afford" to pay them.

Beware the perils of buying too cheap – you will get the suppliers that you deserve, not the suppliers that you need. Always buy the best that you can afford, but ensure you get the very best possible outcome.

7. Create a Win-Win with any supplier

Here's a novel way to look at supplier relationships:

"Treat your suppliers like you would treat your very best customers."

When your suppliers go that extra mile for you - appreciate them. A sincere "Thank You" is often much more than they get from their other customers. A written testimonial will be highly appreciated by their staff.

What you encourage and praise you will tend to get more of.

Key suppliers will usually respond positively to you taking the time and effort to include them as part of your team.

You will meet suppliers who have the potential to produce outcomes that can change your business and your life. The survival or prosperity of your business may be dependent upon certain key suppliers.

These relationships must be managed, so here are some suggestions to help you achieve this:

- Set and maintain standards of behaviour between your business and your suppliers.
- Treat suppliers fairly. Do not assume they will not notice if you do not.
- Help every supplier to help you.

- If they ask you to help them – always do so if you can.
- Where you do not enjoy a good relationship with any key supplier – establish the reasons and make improvements.
- If you get into conflict, do not step away but step in and do your best to solve it with the minimum of hassle.
- Maintain and develop every supplier relationship as needed for them serve you well.
- Where necessary, develop quantitative and qualitative measures to track every supplier relationship.

Every Win-Win with a supplier enables you to Win-Win with your customers.

Delivery strategy challenge four:
How can I get my external team to perform better?

Delivery checklist	Doing this!	Do more!	Start doing!
1: Be clear what outcomes you want from external team			
2: Get internal focus clear before enrolling external team			
3: Test and measure to maximise ROI			
4: Make each supplier a profit centre			
5: Lead your external team			
6: Buy the best suppliers you can afford			
7: Create a Win-Win with suppliers			
TOTAL			

Transfer your totals to the table on Page 311

Delivery strategy challenge five: How can I find more of the right people to help me grow my business?

Most businesses will spend whatever they need to attract as many customers as possible.

But often these businesses struggle to find enough of the right people to deliver what they have sold. And so there is imbalance between the selling and delivery areas.

So how can any business attract enough of the right people? The answer is that employees are buyers just like our customers. We need to sell our employment to them. And once we've sold it, we need to continue to sell it, because we must never forget that our employees are volunteers not hostages.

Here are 7 things to think and do. Try them out and see if they fit. Then choose the ones that work best for you.

1. Be authentic to attract the right people

Attracting enough of the right employees is similar to attracting the right customers. And again, authenticity is key.

If you want to attract a special customer you need a highly attractive offer delivered through effective sales and delivery processes.

Attracting the best talent is just the same. Make your offer sufficiently desirable. Then sell and deliver it to them. You also have to keep it sold by giving constant attention to the relationship. Just like you would with a key customer.

- Be clear about how you do things here (culture) and project this authentically out into the jobs market.
- Be clear about the type of employer you do not want to be.
- And clear about the type of employer you do want to be.

Set up your marketing system to attract enough of the right people to your business.

If necessary, get help from a recruitment specialist to manage your recruitment (marketing) process. Any recruitment specialist will help you navigate the rules of the game you need to know when you advertise, interview, and enrol recruits.

Bear in mind that the team that you recruit ultimately determines what you will achieve in your business. **Buy the best you can afford.**

2. Continually market to every new and current employee

Keep marketing to prospective employees before they even join you. Do not leave a gap after you send them an acceptance letter. You've spent time and effort and you want them to turn up on the date agreed.

Assuming that money is the only incentive can prove an expensive mistake. Every employee has their own agenda for working with you. So, work to understand their motives and what incentives they respond to. Discover the reasons why they get out of bed every day and come to work.

Just like you have customers who return to buy again and again, investigate why your employees keep coming back. Take time to ask individuals why they like to work with you. Ask individuals and the overall team, the two key questions:

- Out of 10 how would you rate working here for you?
- If their answer is short of a 10 (like 8/10) ask them what could make it a 10?

Be realistic and serious here, do not shoot the messenger, and keep the trust going. You will find out some things you would never have known without asking. And you may get some surprises.

But do this right and you will create a more cohesive and enjoyable place to work. And know that you have the team that you deserve. And if they are not the team that you want, then work to improve your employment proposition.

Creating a better place to work attracts and produces a better team. And better teams build better businesses.

3. Define and systematise your recruitment process

There are lots of people out there, and they can't decide if your business is the perfect fit for them. The hiring decision is yours, and you must define each proposition that you are offering to any recruit, and exactly why you need that person.

Be very clear what you want and ensure that you make every prospective recruit as knowledgeable as possible about this. Be open and share this information. Ensure you produce a job specification.

This should include a clear summary of the problems you want your recruit to solve for your business. Be prepared to test them on their ability to solve the type of problems they will meet in their job in your business. Recruitment specialists can usually help you devise ways to achieve this.

This helps any new recruit to hit the ground running on their starting date. You want them contributing to your business as soon as possible to maximise your return on investment.

Explain to candidates that to ensure that you have the best fit, you are slow to hire. Never hire a person if they do not feel right. Ask them to complete some tests or trial period in the job before you fully commit.

Be quick to fire when you employ the wrong person. Just accept that you made a mistake and let them go

Decide your performance standards for your recruitment process and keep refining it until it you employ exactly the recruits that you need.

4. Sell your vision and culture when recruiting

Your business is unique. And your job before you recruit is to establish exactly how it is unique in the eyes of any prospective employee.

Be clear about where are you are now, and be able to explain and paint your picture of where are you going, how you will get there and when.

Be able to explain exactly how the recruit will fit into your plans. The talents they have and how you will help them to use these to progress in your business. Discuss how you see them fitting in and contributing. And discuss what is in it for the recruit.

The recruit is buying your job. Therefore, treat recruiting as a sales process. Also, note that they are selling themselves to you. So, watch and check for any signs that they are not being authentic.

Generate confidence by explaining the job in terms of its challenges and how the recruit's skills match up. Explain how and when you will review their progress after they start with you.

5. Test and measure to keep your team productive

Your team is your most expensive asset. It is also your most productive. To measure how productive, you must find the right KPNs. Take time to do this, because you can't manage what you can't measure.

Start by measuring the outputs. Then drill under these to monitor those specific inputs that produce each output. Explain what you are doing and why, then ask for involvement, ideas and suggestions how you can maintain and improve productivity.

Focus your improvement activities by starting a daily log to note ongoing problems and challenges as they arise. What happened, what was done and why? Then review with your team to discover what can be improved. Create buy-in by discussing and agreeing how individuals and the team can improve productivity.

Flag up any training needs. Agree and plan essential on the job training and coaching. Write systems and "How To?" manuals that:

- Increase productivity and facilitate testing and measuring.
- Decrease the time required for new recruits to reach competence.
- Facilitate cross-training to cover for absences, holidays, overcome bottlenecks and to maintain workflow.
- Maximise output from equipment, IT and technology.

Improving productivity requires constant attention. What you focus on – you will get more of.

6. Encourage every individual to progress as far as they can

As your business grows, there will be more and new problems for you to solve. The more of these that your team solves for you, the more that you can focus on growing your business.

To help your team solve problems for your business, remove any barriers to their growth, and remove any limits on their capability. Help and encourage them to create the tools and learn any skills that they need to do a better job.

Never allow your team to limit the growth of your business. Be realistic on your and their expectations. What they can and cannot do. Give everyone the opportunity to progress as far as they can or want to. But be aware that expecting them to progress too far will prove counter-productive.

Effective education and training pays huge dividends not only from up-skilling, but also from improved motivation and involvement. Adopt a policy of "Learn to Earn". As individuals are prepared to learn more, make sure that they have opportunity to earn more.

Set *Goldilocks Goals* – not too much and not too little. Just enough to progress, but not too much to overwhelm. Train all the time (and that includes you). And as your business grows be sure to share the outcomes.

7. Reward everyone in your team

Creating the very best jobs that you can afford will attract your best team. Increasing your profits allows you to create better jobs. And increasing productivity generates more profits and so on.

Improving the performance of your business is your number one job. If you don't do this, neither will anyone else. Work with your team to improve productivity, celebrate the outcomes, and share the successes.

Praise and reward both individual and team performance. Focus on and eliminate unacceptable performance.

Use test and measure to find those KPNs that allow you and your team to monitor performance in real time. The older the numbers, the less use they are. KPNs may be quantitative or qualitative.

Become highly innovative at using both financial and non-financial rewards to stretch you and your team. Productivity is always encouraged with the right mix of learning and earning.

Know that it is within your capability to build the dream team that you could never afford to buy.

"One Team – One Dream"
Kevin Roberts – Worldwide CEO of Saatchi and Saatchi

Delivery strategy challenge five: How can I find more of the right people to help me grow my business?

Delivery checklist	Doing this!	Do more!	Start doing!
1: Be authentic to attract the right people			
2: Continually market to your employees			
3: Define and systematise recruitment process			
4: Sell your vision and culture when recruiting			
5: Test and measure to keep your team productive			
6: Encourage every individual to progress as far as they can			
7: Reward everyone in your team			
TOTAL			

Transfer your totals to the table on Page 311

Delivery strategy challenge six: How can I get better customers who pay more?

Here we explore how you can maximise the impact of your delivery process upon changing and improving your relationships with your customers. Maximising the impact of your selling process upon customers is covered in the sales strategy section.

Your selling team has sold your promise to your customers and now your delivery process must deliver that promise in full and satisfy every customer.

There may opportunities for you to provide more value for your customers. You may include this in your current offer. But you may also develop product or service offers that your customers find valuable enough to pay more for them.

Here are 7 things to think and do. Try them out and see if they fit. Then choose the ones that work best for you.

1. Investigate your delivery process for ways to increase your sales revenue

The current profit and all the other results now being produced by your business is the result of you using all current resources.

Start to investigate your delivery process by listing every part of your delivery process. If this is different by price or customer segment, then split your list accordingly. You are working to get clear what you are doing to satisfy your clients.

The next step is to evaluate and write down at each step of your process, how that activity adds value to your promise. You are looking for steps that cost your business, but don't add proportionate value to your product or service.

For example: You may pride yourself on next day delivery and spend extra money on this. But it may not be that important to a large proportion of your customers. Therefore, you are over-satisfying these clients.

Look at every client contact point. Every discussion with every client. Every point of value transfer. Every written and spoken client connection. Do you give additional information, tips or advice in your conversations and correspondence with clients?

Get everything written down and then examine each delivery process for what you are doing and why. Do not understate what you do. Everything you do costs resources. And you are looking for opportunities to exploit these resources for extra profit.

In this process avoid any tendency to underestimate what we do and overestimate what our clients do. Make sure you include every point of customer service, what you do when customers complain, and what happens when you go that extra mile for some clients.

If your business attracts online comments on websites such as Trip Advisor, check what your clients are saying about you and your competitors.

Gather information on your delivery process and look for all ways that you add value to the lives of your clients. It's likely that you will see immediate ways to increase your sales revenue and margins.

2. Always put your clients at the centre of everything you do

Look around in the business world and how infrequently you see an optimum match between what any business supplies and the needs of its clients. For extreme cases of this look at our public services where a close match is very rare. It is also rare in banking and most other financial services.

Thus, when you put your clients at the centre of everything you do, you will stand out. That's in every selling, delivery and financial process that impacts your clients.

Your business exists only to satisfy your clients, so take every opportunity to add value to them and profit to you. Work with your clients to better understand their needs and how you can service them.

Being authentic builds trust and enables a closer relationship with each client

Look for barriers and reasons why clients don't buy more from you. Work to eliminate or reduce these. Help clients to your solution. And always help them to get to their solution.

Bear in mind two important maxims:

- Customers are much more value conscious than price conscious.
- Customers want to feel more important, listened to and understood.

For these reasons speed is highly important when dealing with clients. If you promise to call a client back within the hour or 24 hours, make sure you do so. Expect that they will notice if you don't.

3. Make space by culling your customers

In any business, there are usually customers who are "more trouble than they are worth".

If you have any of these they will consume more than their fair share of your resources and generate less than their fair share of profit.

They will *"know the price of everything and the value of nothing"*. Often these are the high hassle clients who are most fussy and complain most about your prices and service.

List your clients and then rate them. We use the following designations suggested in a seminar attended years ago:

A. **Awesome:** These clients love you and refer others to your business.
B. **Basic:** Your everyday clients who turn up and buy from you.
C. **Can't Deal With:** These are the customers that you either shift onto being a B-type customer or you cull them.
D. **Dead:** You should not be dealing with these. Cull them immediately.

Be realistic – where are you wasting your resources? Who are your price conscious clients? Who gives you most hassle and complain most?

Set objectives to free up resources by shifting the C-type clients and culling the Ds.

Find ways to go the extra mile to delight and uplift your A and B clients. And create objectives to use freed up resources to target and attract more A and B-type clients to generate extra profit.

4. Regularly ask for feedback from clients

Most of us have a tendency to serve our clients and then leave them well alone.

"If it ain't broke – don't fix it."

We avoid drawing our client into any dialogue about our relationship with them. That is until we notice that they have been lured elsewhere and deserted us. At which point it's a bit late.

There is huge opportunity to be gained by being closer to clients. The closer you are, the less price conscious they will be. They have a low tendency to look elsewhere, happy in their habit to keep buying from you. But you must maintain their habit by maintaining the closeness.

The first activity to create closeness is simple appreciation. And the easiest appreciation to give to clients is the simple "Thank you for your business". And this is often neglected. You can speak it, write it, shout it – whatever. But make sure that you do it.

Another way is to ask, "How else can we serve you?". This opens a dialogue where you may be able to help them further. Or if you cannot service their needs, advise them where they could be served.

Timing is important. When you have delighted them is a good time to engage in this type of dialogue.

Barriers are down between you and them and you are both relaxed and open. They will be frank at these times if you ask the right questions in the right ways. Here is when they will tell you some good stuff.

Get your questions ready to gather information. Start with:

- What they think of you
- What they are doing now
- Their future needs
- Their current unmet needs
- Your competitors
- What they think of the market and trends

Work out which areas are most important to you and write out your specific questions. Then ask as many as you can before this opportunity passes.

Don't be afraid to ask the "Out of 10" question. Ask them: "Out of 10, how would you rate your experience of buying from us?"

Make sure they give you a frank answer. Be prepared to quiz them further until they do. Then ask them: "What would make it a 10?"

You may get some really useful information from engaging with your customers. Not asking gets you none.

You want to know what you do well. But extra profit lies in doing these things better and how to get them better is by using effective dialogue with customers.

There may be opportunity from those things that you could do but don't. Because you have never asked your clients for this information. By engaging and asking you can usually unearth some serious opportunities

5. Know your numbers for customers, products, services and margins

The correct KPNs never lie. They have no opinions, no axe to grind, are logical and unambiguous. Yet one of the main limits on business success is the inability of the team to make consistently correct decisions. And KPNs facilitate decision making.

Apply the 80/20 rule to your customers: 80% of customers produce 20% of profits. And 20% of customers produce 80% of profits. You may not see exactly 80/20 but you will probably see a disproportionate profit produced by the majority of your customers.

This is also the case for products and services. Focus on those customers and products that produce these disproportional results.

- Can you sell and deliver more to these customers?
- Can you sell more of these products into your market?
- Is it economical and profitable for you to achieve this?

In his book, *Great by Choice*, Jim Collins mentions that you should always "fire bullets before firing cannonballs". He explains that we must reduce risk by never making big changes until we have taken time to analyse our choices. Select and sample the improvements into our market. Then test and re-measure the results, before doing them wholesale.

Use numbers analysis to decide the customers (and suppliers) you want to work with now and future. Apply this also in the areas of customer service, and every part of your product and service delivery system.

Look for opportunities to eliminate waste and generate extra profit. The more profit you make – the more profit you can make.

6. Always look for more value to add

We have never encountered a business that has the perfect and most profitable match between its customers and the products or services it provides. There is always opportunity. And if you can't yet see it, then analysis provides you with the knowledge to find and provide it.

If you genuinely cannot find opportunities to provide extra value at greater return to your business, our suggestion is that you discuss this with a qualified consultant. Whether they confirm you are correct or they help you locate opportunities, it's a guaranteed win.

Regularly check out your competitors for their new offers. Look in other industries and markets for ideas to use in your business. Attend seminars and workshops. If you don't look – you will never find.

Always do your numbers before launching new offers. Then test these with clients who will provide accurate and relevant feedback.

Use this feedback to modify your offers, if possible re-test with the same clients. And then do this with clients who have not sampled your first offer.

Gather information before committing your resources to wholesale launch. You will gather information as you sell your new offers, and as you deliver them. Both processes provide opportunity to discover how you can add even more value to your products, services and relationships.

Your business exists to supply value at a profit. Explore all opportunities to guarantee this.

7. Expand your number of offers without increasing costs

There are many examples of companies selling premium products. These are liked by their buyers because they produce an extra value that resonates with them.

Visitors to Disneyland will pay extra for a ticket where they do not have to queue for rides and facilities. When Disney launched this, it generated an instant extra profit, at negligible cost to Disney.

So, there is usually opportunity in any business to deliver a premium product at an extra cost. The benefits of this premium product must be clearly defined. So, that the buyer can weigh these benefits against the increased price. Remember, customers are not price conscious, they are value conscious

Where the buyer rejects the premium product, test and measure their responses. Then it is up to the seller to adjust their offer with even more value to tempt the buyer.

In addition to launching a premium product, there is often an opportunity to add extra services, or other value onto existing standard products.

There may even be opportunity to strip back a standard product to provide an economy product. Because this lowers the costs, and price, these economy products can provide access to new market segments and produce major profits.

This exercise is all about generating extra sales revenue and greater overall profit. Your delivery process will usually provide good opportunity to explore what you can do to provide more value to your clients and make them feel more important.

In all your dealings with clients, take every opportunity to improve the fit between you and them. Analyse what you could do and get your questions ready for when you engage clients.

This eventually allows you to achieve a *Category of One* relationship. The match is so good that they will always ask you first. You will be top of mind. And they will not go elsewhere until they are sure that you cannot help them.

See more about this in the book by Jim Calloway, *Category of One*.

There is a virtuous circle to helping and serving your clients and the wider world. Take time to explore this. Whatever you put out there will come back, in some way shape or form.

Here's a final thought to consider:

"I don't know what your destiny will be, but one thing I do know: The only ones among you who will be truly happy are those who will have sought and found how to serve."

Albert Schweitzer

Delivery strategy challenge six: How can I get better customers who pay more?

Delivery checklist	Doing this!	Do more!	Start doing!
1: Investigate delivery process for ways to increase sales revenue			
2: Always put clients at the centre			
3: Make space by culling customers			
4: Regularly ask for feedback			
5: Know your KPNs			
6: Always look for more value to add			
7: Expand offers without increasing costs			
TOTAL			

Transfer your totals to the table on Page 311

Delivery strategy challenge seven: How can I grow my business faster but stay in control?

Here are 7 things to think and do. Try them out and see if they fit. Then choose the ones that work best for you.

1. **Decide exactly why you must grow and by how much**

For every hour that you plan, you'll save many more in execution. Be clear why you need to grow, by how much and by when.

What personal goals will you fulfil with your growth plan? How will your lifestyle be changed? What will you be able to enjoy that you cannot enjoy right now? Will you be happier? In what ways?

It may be that the needs of your business are driving your wish to grow:

- You may need to increase scale to maintain or develop an improved foothold or control in your market. And not doing this may be a threat to your business.
- Your business may currently have a weakness that you must overcome to consolidate it further. You may need a key member of staff, maybe a piece of key equipment or other facility that requires you to grow.
- It may be that your reason is simply to generate more profit to provide more working capital to take advantage of an opportunity. To increase sales, add additional products or services, to buy stock, equipment etc.

Be clear about your reasons. Then it's time to look at what barriers you may have to overcome. A simple SWOT analysis would prove useful:

Strengths:
Ones already in your business, or that you may need to develop to achieve your plan.

Weaknesses:
That you have now and need to overcome.

Opportunities:
That you have right now or that you expect will arise from the changes that you intend to make.

Threats:
That are now current or that you expect to encounter from the changes you intend to make.

It is far better to set off with some analysis of what future barriers you may need to overcome. Rather than wait until you need to deal with them in real time.

2. Know that it starts with you

Know that a bigger business means more challenges to solve. And the way that you achieve this is to build a team that helps you solve these challenges with minimum involvement from you. This allows you to focus your capabilities on building the business.

It is 100% your job to build and lead your team. Your management and leadership will be tested. How do you feel about that personal challenge? How big can you grow?

A good starting point is to list your tasks under the following headings:

- **Time consuming tasks:** Those that take up lots of your time.

- **Stressful tasks:** Those you find stressful
- **Productive tasks:** The ones where you know that you are most productive
- **Happy tasks**: The ones that you are happy to do.

You will note those tasks for which you do not have passion or natural ability. The ones to do less of and delegate to others who are more talented and suited.

You will also note tasks where you are highly productive and that energise you. The ones you want to do more of.

Get clear about those tasks that you want to do more of and less of. Those you want to stop doing. And any that you want to start doing. This will help you get clear about where your talents are best used and what type of skills and abilities you must look for in your current and future team.

You will gain valuable insights into what new talent you must attract into your team. Start with you, knowing that no one else will build the team that builds your dream.

3. Establish financial targets and milestones

These are about "How much" and "By when" and specify expected profit, cashflow, sales, costs and so on. Of course, these are just a best guess from looking at today's data. But you will flag up any future challenges by creating a financial model for your business now and throughout your intended growth phase.

The definition of financial modelling:

"The construction of spreadsheet models that illustrate a company's likely financial results in quantitative terms."

Using a financial model is like looking into the future. You can investigate every one of your assumptions for minimal cost and absolutely no risk using "What happens if"? analysis:

- How much working capital will you need to fuel the expansion?
- Where will you get the additional working capital?
- If you run short of cash – what options do you have?
- What will be the impact of increased fixed costs such as more space, more people, more equipment or technology and so on.

Estimate the costs of anything you will need to achieve your plan and look at the impact of these on your business.

If you require additional funding from your bank or from outside investors, you will be asked to produce financial models for your business that show your cashflow forecast profit and loss, and revenue and cost budgets.

Your lender will use these to assess their risk, as they study what you have included and whether this is a fair scenario of what could play out.

4. Test and measure to find weak spots

Use financial modelling to investigate what happens when you expand your sales by 20%, 40% and so on.

Look for the impacts upon cashflow, and the selling and delivery processes. At what time and place will you need to employ more individuals. How will this impact profitability? And so on.

Use this modelling to get a good feel for what is coming up and what steps you would take to solve the challenges. Involve your team as you build and solve these "What if" scenarios. And don't forget to include qualitative measures.

Growth involves rapid change and some people are not suited to this. Think through the steps you would take. Make sure that you can maintain standards as you deliver more promises. Be prepared in areas such as customer service.

Look for potential imbalances between people, systems and equipment. Identify where training may be needed. Who would supply this?

Plan well and test every assumption before it may become real and need to be dealt with urgently.

*"**EVERY** minute you **SPEND** in **PLANNING SAVES 10** minutes in **EXECUTION**; this gives you a 1,000 percent Return on Energy!"*

Brian Tracey

5. Plan your people needs

In business, what people will do and not do, achieve and shy away from, are great unknowns. You never know until it happens. So, sooner or later you need to throw the switch.

And selling is usually the first switch. We liken this to putting your foot on the accelerator in a car. That's when you really see what the car can do.

Don't spend too much time worrying about the strengths and weaknesses of your team. If you have glaring omissions and weaknesses, then address these before any expansion. But don't allow paralysis by analysis. Test them and you may be surprised.

Most businesses have spare capacity to increase sales without increasing the number of people on the team. Once you expand your sales, any cracks will start to show. If you've done your planning homework, you will know what to do. Do it fast and do it well.

You will also see the beginnings of future problems and it is these that you start planning for as you push forward.

Cover for your personal and team challenges quickly so that these do not stall your progress. Take every step to improve current team performance to the maximum, before hiring anyone new. Hire more staff when your people are screaming for help. Avoid hiring in front of demand.

But don't assume that employing more people is the only answer to any expansion challenges. This is a common and expensive trap.

Let your team be tested and challenged. This overcomes weakness and builds sustainable strength. Where any individual struggles with a job that is just too big, be prepared to split their job. Do the stop/start and more/less exercise described in Point 2 above to guide them into jobs that satisfy and energise them.

Do everything possible to prepare yourself and your team for change. Do your homework and know that whatever comes up, you will deal with it.

6. Use targeted incentives

To encourage the motivation and openness to change, be prepared to share the results from growing your business.

Your financial model shows you your gains from growth and you can use these numbers to calculate how much you will share and by when. Never compromise your cash flow with overgenerous incentives.

Instead, focus incentives on those areas where you want the biggest improvements: sales, delivery or finance.

Use incentives to get your team to find innovative and inventive solutions. Define the challenges and incentivise them to find solutions.

Keep things simple throughout. If things become complex, then simplify them.
There must be a definite outcome and a clear incentive for producing the outcome. Do not fudge.

Where time is needed for the results to show up, keep your team engaged and informed about the progress, or otherwise, that is being achieved. Of course, incentives are about much more than money. Different individuals are encouraged by different things.

Talk to your team, ask them what they would like from your business. Use your skills to arrive at those incentives that suit both them and you.

Know that results depend upon performance and performance depends upon training and development. Use the promise of incentives to encourage your team to up-skill. To create volunteers and not hostages.

Never backslide on incentives. The key to incentives are communication, invention, consistency and regular review. Get the right incentives in place and your business will fly. They are a high upside and low downside investment when you get them right. Take all steps to ensure that they remain closely matched to your business and your team.

7. Ask for customer feedback to select areas of focus

Every business has limited resources to satisfy their customers. These resources must be supplied at a profit to the business. So, the key objective is to maximise return on these resources and a good place to start is by applying the 80/20 rule:

Use the 80/20 to look for disproportionate results within your product and service segments. Look for those clients and products that provide disproportionate profits.

You may not see exactly 20% of your products creating 80% of profits. Or 20% of your clients providing 80% of profits. But you will see some disproportionate effects.

And you will achieve greater profit by focusing more of your resources on achieving more of these disproportionate results.

Those customers and products which provide the best returns also provide your focus for the introduction of new and improved products. This is achieved by asking those customers what else they would like to buy. What other problems would they like to have solved?

You have a focus for engagement, so just ask the right questions that allow you to match higher margin products to your newly discovered customer wants and needs. Make your business client centric around your 20% most profitable customers. Get very close to these people.

Remember that people don't buy what they need, they buy what they want. Be smart in asking them the right questions to discover what they want, and make sure that your offer fulfils their needs as closely as possible.

Take away their reasons not to buy from you. Do not sell to them – just let them buy. Create and deliver promises just for them, make sure they get the right quality of customer service.

Take these clients as your barometer. Listen to their comments and complaints. What else is going on in their lives? Can your business help? Can you help them on their way to another solution?

Never stop asking about the value they want to buy. They are important to your business, let them feel that, they will keep coming back, and they will become your raving fans.

Delivery strategy challenge seven:
How can I grow my business faster but stay in control?

Delivery checklist	**Doing this!**	**Do more!**	**Start doing!**
1: Decide why you must grow and by how much			
2: Know that it starts with you			
3: Establish financial targets and milestones			
4: Test and measure to find weak spots			
5: Plan your people needs			
6: Use targeted incentives			
7: Ask for customer feedback			
TOTAL			

Transfer your totals to the table on Page 311

Part 5

Financial strategy Seven x7

Seven common challenges in financial strategy

Financial strategy Seven x7

Seven common challenges in financial strategy

So, last but by no means least, we come to look at finances. The numbers, the boring numbers. Except they are not boring, they are the heart of your business. Without the right numbers, you have no business.

Or very soon will have no business.

You need to know your numbers in order to make the right decisions, and to know that decisions that you've already made are working out correctly.

If you are not a numerate person, then you must employ someone who is. This will usually be your accountant or bookkeeper. They will help you generate and interpret your numbers.

The minimum that you must do is to understand what your numbers are telling you and what decisions they indicate that you must make.

In any market, you have competitors, and if they produce and use their numbers and you do not, then you are severely disadvantaged.

And if you have the advantage of knowing and using your numbers, then it's likely that it's they who will be trying to catch up with you.

So, here are some ways to approach your numbers and get them working for you.

Financial strategy challenge one: The basics

Business owners too often avoid the numbers. You do so at your peril.

Your business has to produce numbers to report to HMRC in order to calculate income and employment taxes. Also for you to pay the correct amount of VAT.

Now, since you need to pay to produce these numbers anyway, then you may as well use them to generate income for your business. So, how can you do that?

Here are 7 things to try out. Give all of them a go and choose the ones that work best for you.

1. Develop your financial strategy

You will have a strategy for your business. This may be formal like a written business plan, but you may also be carrying your strategy around in your head.

If you don't have a strategy set down in some shape or form, then you may be going around in circles. And certainly, not operating your business as effectively as you could to generate maximum profit and benefit to you.

Like it or avoid it, money is the lifeblood of your business.

How will your business generate cash? What sales activities will you undertake to create this cash? How will you spend your money to generate growth? How much money will you take as your salary?

Your financial strategy will provide the answers to these questions and more. Do not hold back from asking your accountant to help with this. You may find it difficult, but it is easy for them to help you get started on developing a sound financial strategy for your business.

Take this a step at a time and don't move forward until you fully understand the relevance of each component of your strategy to the relevant part of your business.

As your business develops, you will discover this to be excellent use of your time.

2. Connect finance with your business goals

The starting point is, of course, your business goals. Some business owners struggle with getting these clear and writing them down. If you find it difficult, then get professional help.

Would you turn up at the airport check-in counter not having booked your flight? And just tell the check-in assistant to send you on any flight where they have seats?

Of course you wouldn't - you would plan your holiday by booking your flights and accommodation. You'd pack your bags, get your currency and so on.

Now if you do all this just for your holiday, then why not apply the same diligence to writing down your business goals and giving some thought as to how these will show up in your numbers?

Henry Ford famously said, "For every hour I spend in planning, I save ten hours in execution". Take his advice and think through where your business is heading before spending your scarce resources and not afterwards.

What numbers will your strategy produce? Will there be enough profit to pay your costs and provide a worthwhile return on your effort? Will your strategy produce enough cash-flow to fund the growth of your business? Or will you need to borrow additional funds?

If you have not already done this for your business, get started right away and you will immediately improve your probability of success.

3. Develop a financial model for your business

The best way to ensure that decisions turn out correct is to produce a financial model of your business. This does not need to be complex, but will involve you calculating some simple numbers and making some basic assumptions.

- What will be your sales revenue?
- How much will you spend to produce this?
- How much profit will these activities produce?

Or just talk to your accountant and ask him/her to produce you a financial model for your business. One that is accurate enough to allow you to check the impact of your decisions *before* you put them into action.

Ask your accountant to find your main business driver(s) and explain how your financial model produces these drivers. To monitor your business day-to-day you then only need to focus on these main drivers. You will know that when these drivers are good, so is your profitability and cash flow.

Get started with your financial model. Initially it does not need to be overly complicated or even 100% accurate. You don't even need to understand it fully.

When something does not go to plan, just pick up the phone to your accountant and ask them to check your financial model and tell you what you must adjust to bring it back on track. In this way, your financial model will set you a clear direction, and keep you pointing in that direction.

4. Produce good financial information

In far too many businesses, good financial information is produced once a year at the year-end, and just to externally account to HMRC.

It is impossible to manage your business effectively only by looking back after your year-end. Ideally you require information to be in real time. The faster that you can see what is happening, the easier it is for you to make accurate decisions to keep your business on track.

The key here is to match the provision of your financial information to the rate of change within your business. If your revenue and costs change quickly, then you need to see the impact of these changes as fast as possible, in order to make decisions about pricing, selling and buying etc.

There is often a belief that some decisions need to be made without reference to accurate information. There is no time to wait – I must act now. The first time you have to act without having the right information, watch out for the outcome. And for the next decision-making occasion make sure that you have the right information to hand. Give yourself every advantage to manage your business.

At least identify and know your daily, weekly, and monthly business financial drivers. When these are on track, chances are that everything else is working correctly.

When these key drivers go off track, then consult your business financial model and look for the causes. If you struggle to identify the causes, then consult your accountant and ask them to compare your current numbers with your financial model. And then advise you what to do next.

It is advisable to record monthly, weekly even daily information to allow you to provide information for external accounting. Reviewing this will help you to manage your business accurately.

As an absolute minimum, you need to record sales, debtors, creditors, upcoming receipts and upcoming payments. To make accurate decisions about sales you must know your most profitable products and your most profitable clients. To manage staff costs you need to generate data on the effectiveness and efficiency of your staff.

Explain to your financial team why you want specific information and let them produce it for you. If your business requires fast and extensive information you will need to employ your own bookkeeper or accountant.

5. Order your financial priorities

Is this how you think your financial priorities should run? You make sales and you pay all your operational costs, including payments to yourself. Then whatever is left is profit and you can pay yourself more or invest it to improve your business.

No - you cannot do it like that.

You must use these profits to improve the financial well-being of your business in the following ways:

Account for taxes

If your business is producing a surplus, then you will be liable to pay some type of business income tax. If you employ people you must pay some kind of employment taxes.

And if you add VAT to your invoices, then you are collecting taxes on behalf of HMRC. This money is not yours and you should keep it separate from your normal cash flow.

Avoid trouble from the tax collectors by making sure you have their money ready when you need to make payments.

Reduce borrowings

Make regular payments to reduce any borrowings or other business debt. Debt may be a necessary cost within your business, but aim to make regular debt reductions. Immediately this reduces the costs of your debt and also makes things easier if and when you need to borrow in the future.

Build up reserves

Whenever possible, make regular payments into your business reserve account. Most businesses have very limited cash reserves and if emergencies arise they find things really difficult.

A good start is to save up at least two months of your total outgoing expenses. Save more If you trade in an unpredictable business environment.

Then, whatever money remains, you can pay yourself.

Note:

It is important for your business to pay you at least the 'market rate' for the job that you do. You do not serve your business by paying yourself last, only paying yourself what is left after everyone and everything else has been paid.

The importance of your personal well-being cannot be overstated. You must structure your business so that it can always pay you, and always pay you first and not last.

6. Set up your staff as profit centres

When you know that everyone employed in your business, including you, is making a profit for your business, then you will have a profitable business

Every member of staff, including yourself, must produce more money than they cost the business. Or they must produce a saving for the business that is greater than their cost to the business. Otherwise, your business is better off without them.

Starting with your most expensive team members (this could be you) find and compare the total costs and the profit generated by each individual.

This is relatively easy for sales individuals where the sales revenue produced and the cost incurred to produce this revenue are readily available.

The profitability of sales support staff and administration staff is not usually so easy to define. You will need to make some assumptions and then check and adapt these over subsequent months. A suggestion here is to calculate the costs for every support staff member and then allocate this cost proportionately to the individuals that they support.

For example: Susan is a general admin person. She spends 70% of her time supporting Denise, the admin manager, 30% of her time supporting the MD and 20% of her time supporting the sales director. Her costs would therefore be allocated to each of these individuals in line with these percentages.

Once you have established your cost and profit centres, you have a benchmark for each individual. Now you have created the opportunity to use this information to improve the productivity of each individual in your team.

7. Interaction with your accountant

Your accountant is a key person within your team. Make sure that he/she also produces a profit for you. It is perfectly OK for you to visit another accountant from time to time to check on the quality of their work. Accountants are not infallible; they make mistakes and omissions. And usually it is you who will pay the price for these.

You are buying a professional service. Make sure you are buying the best that you can afford. If you are one of the many business owners who sees their accountant once a year to review the business numbers for the last 12 months, then it will probably be advantageous to employ a different accountant.

You will obtain the best service and value for money by being proactive with your accountant. Check your numbers before you meet and look for questions that you would like to ask and points you need to discuss.

By meeting regularly, you will develop your knowledge of your numbers and how they relate to your business. Your accountant will study your numbers and will highlight problem areas, challenges or opportunities for you both to discuss.

Start by focusing on these areas and ask them to help you understand the relevant numbers - what to look for and where to find the right information to help you best manage the issue.

Know and understand your key business drivers and how these are calculated. Also, the key factors in your business that you need to manage to influence these drivers

Expect your accountant to help you with all aspects of your business strategy and decision making; to help you find the numbers that tell you how your business is performing; and what to focus on to increase productivity and profitability

Your accountant is not just there for reducing your tax and making statutory returns. They are a key member of your team, should you decide to treat them as such.

Do not be afraid to ask. Here, as in most walks of life, there is just one stupid question. That is the question that you think of, but don't ask.

Financial strategy challenge one: The basics

Financial checklist	Doing this!	Do more!	Start doing!
1: Develop your financial strategy			
2: Connect finance with your business goals			
3: Develop a financial model for your business			
4: Produce good financial information			
5: Order your financial priorities			
6: Set up your staff as profit centres			
7: Interact with your accountant			
TOTAL			

Transfer your totals to the table on Page 312

Financial strategy challenge two: Overcome your numerophobia

When discussing their numbers with business owners, it is clear that many of them avoid looking at their numbers, even when their accountant or bookkeeper presents them to them regularly. It is evident that many people are scared of dealing with the numbers.

They do not seem to know where to start to overcome this and make their numbers their friends. They find them complicated and because they do not have the necessary skills to interpret them, they write them off as meaningless.

Now that is OK. But when your competitors are better at interpreting and using their numbers than you are, then you are at a distinct disadvantage.

Thus, avoiding your numbers cannot be a long-term option if you want your business to prosper.

Here are 7 things to try out. Give all of them a go and choose the ones that work best for you.

1. Don't avoid the numbers

Get acquainted with the idea that your business numbers are your friend and not your enemy. Start to embrace them. Do this by starting to become more articulate around them. Learn the language: cash-flow; profitability; gross margin; revenue; costs and so on.

If you want to stay in business, you can't ignore or avoid your numbers. They are essential to the running of your business. You must learn to be more comfortable with them yourself. And this is the case even when you outsource them to someone else who will produce them, help you interpret them, and guide you to make the correct decisions which your numbers indicate that you should take.

If you don't understand your numbers or you are an avoider, your first step here is to employ someone to produce your key financial information and then filter and translate this down into the essential information that you require for your decision making.

For example, all businesses have Key Performance Numbers (KPNs). These are the most important numbers that tell you how your business is performing.

To explain, just suppose that you owned a body car repair shop. You may focus on the KPN of "How many hours billed today".

Now, would this be a really useful KPN to know, in real time, to communicate to your staff? It's a number – but it's a very important number. It's readily available, easily understood, easy to communicate and no-one needs to avoid it. It can be your friend.

You may post this to all staff during each day. Everyone will know how many hours you need to bill to break even, and how many hours you expect to bill under normal conditions.

There are similar KPNs in your business too. All you need to do is decide that you will locate them and make them your friend. Your bookkeeper or accountant will help. And you will make some new friends.

2. Put your school view of numbers behind you

So many people come out of school hating maths. This then colours their perspective of numbers for the rest of their lives. Yet your business numbers have very little to do with the maths you were taught at school.

You don't need to be personally able to add and subtract, to double entry bookkeep and reconcile your bank account etc. These, and the majority of calculations and equations, are now done by IT systems and computers, with some inputs from your bookkeeper and/or your accountant.

You must produce accounts for submission and possible inspection by HMRC. And so this basic number crunching has to be done.

But it's your business, your investment and your lifestyle that is dictated by your numbers.

And this is why you must be prepared to learn how to interpret your numbers. You must understand what they mean. What message they tell you.

Again, your bookkeeper and/or accountant will help you interpret what your numbers are telling you. And they will help you to make the decisions that subsequently you must make.

I, that's Phil, was rubbish at maths at school. It took me three attempts to pass O-level maths. And even now I can't accurately add up a list of numbers. But I get my accountant to set up the numbers so that my system adds them up into a standard format. And I am now really good at interpreting what this processed information tells me I must do.

Don't let your numbers, or lack of them, intimidate you. Just get the right help to systematise and interpret them. This will make a huge difference to decision making and your business.

3. Know what financial questions to ask

Running a business is like driving a car. Knowing how the engine works and what the different valves and pistons do is certainly useful at times. But it's not essential to driving the car.

Unless you are especially talented at processing your numbers, I plead with you to employ someone to bash through the mechanics of your numbers.

However, as a driver, you need to know which pedal to push to go faster, what you need to do to go slower and so on.

Your numbers underpin everything and will tell you exactly what is happening in your business. And they indicate where you must make decisions and often, how you must implement these to produce a more desirable outcome from your business activities.

But how do you know what to look at first when looking at your numbers? And what are the questions that your numbers indicate that you must ask?

Throughout the rest of this section, we'll illustrate some specific areas where your numbers are particularly important to the health of your business and your personal financial success.

Start with the No 1 challenge you now have in your business. This may be cash-flow. It may be that you need to scale up the business and are looking for the starting place to do this. You may be looking at your pricing. Introducing a new product or line. Managing your way into a new market.

Then write down and ask "How do I...?" questions around this area. Do get second opinions from others in your management team, financial team or your accountant.

As you do this you will find that this No 1 challenge leads naturally onto your No 2 challenge. Proceed the same with that onto your No 3 challenge and so on until you know what numbers you will need to take the right decisions, get things moving, and monitor the results on track.

Then manage your process with full confidence that the numbers produced will indicate where you are, what is happening, and what to do next.

4. Find easier ways to understand the numbers

You may have noticed that you do not necessarily need to be able to write or be at all fluent in say, French, to be able to understand what is being said by a waiter in a restaurant or a shop owner. If you do not know what they mean, you can ask questions of them and guess their meaning until you understand enough to proceed.

And this is true when working with and understanding your numbers. You tell your bookkeeper and/or accountant the challenge where you need financial information. They dig it out and present it to you. You ask them questions until you find the answers you are looking for. At this stage, you have the option to check your conclusion with them.

If they feel that your planned decision may be slightly off, then they (and you) can dig some more and so on until you share the conclusion, decision and course of action. Then you can get on with implementation.

In order to do this, you only need to understand the basics. But gradually you will improve your understanding and expertise. The trick here is not to feel overwhelmed by what feels like their deep understanding and your seeming ignorance. You will get better and you will be surprised how fast this will happen when you proceed in this way.

Think about the last time you went on a foreign holiday. Did you return knowing lots more words and phrases than when you started out? And so it is with your numbers. Just be patient with yourself and trust yourself to work things through. You may be very surprised how quickly your numeracy improves.

And remember: "There is only one stupid question, the one that you think of but don't ask."

5. Manage your money

If you write any meaningful business goals, most of them will be of the "How much and by when" format.

- The income from my business will be X by when Y.
- I will increase my sales by A by when B.
- I will increase my average price for every product/service by 10% before 31st December this year (specifying an exact date).

The lifeblood of your business is your cash-flow, and this is a logical first place to start. How much cash will come into my business, where will it flow next, and by when?

It is not a sound move to receive your money into your bank account and then let it flow out without managing how much and by when. It is much more advisable to receive the cash, having already prioritised, planned and apportioned how much is going here or there and by when.

Key destinations for your cash will vary depending upon your type of business, but you will usually have to apportion cash to the following:

- Wages, salaries and employment taxes
- Corporation tax, income tax and VAT
- Suppliers (creditors)
- Stock and Work-In-Progress (WIP)
- Debt repayment
- Cash reserves for longer term spending

Along with optional allocations to:

- Invest in the growth of your business
- Increase your knowledge, skills and abilities
- Staff training and development

And it's usually a smart move to save some cash for rainy day contingencies.

Again, your bookkeeper and/or accountant will help you identify the key areas for your business and help you set up the optimal system for long term monitoring of income and outgoings.

The outcome you want here is to have the right amount of cash available when you need to spend it. The more that you ensure this, the easier and more effective will be your management of the business.

6. Look for financial improvements

When I look at the financial situation of many small business, I note that many business owners seem to have some kind of resistance to making too much money. They give too much 'value' for the prices they charge. They let customers pay late and allow suppliers to overcharge.

I tell them, it is your business, it is your social and commercial risk, it is your lifestyle, and it is your future. You did not go into your own business to be worse off than being in a job – did you?

It is your right and purpose to make as much money from your business as possible. You are not a charity. If you are charitable, make the money from your business first and then give to others. Do not give your money to customers. If they are willing, allow them to pay as much as they will.

ALWAYS be looking for ways to make more money out of your business. Check your numbers to look for ways to increase prices, to add more value (and price) to your offers.

And never forget to look for lower costs and greater efficiencies throughout every activity in your business.

- Can you reduce your selling costs to existing clients?
- Can you reduce your selling costs to gain new clients?
- Is it possible to deliver the same product or service for less cost?
- How feasible is it to reduce overall costs? Energy, utilities, telephone, wages, taxes, materials.

Stay on the lookout for cost reductions and ways to increase revenue. Include your staff and suppliers in this. Ask them for ideas and suggestions and they will buy into the changes.

Be very clear: "The purpose of any business is to make a profit."

Use your numbers to focus your actions and get feedback on your implementation. Think of it this way: Would you like to work 50 hours per week for £40,000 a year? Or work 50 hours per week for £100,000 a year?

Increasing the income from your business is not about working harder, it is about working smarter. And the way that you start right now and continue to work smarter is by understanding and using your numbers.

7. Keep on top of your numbers

Too many business owners do not monitor their numbers on a monthly, three monthly, or even an annual basis.

They collect bills and invoices in their files and give these to their accountant at their financial year end. The accountant goes away and does their computations and 3 to 6 months into the following year, just before the numbers need to be reported to HMRC, he/she comes back with accurate numbers for the whole year.

These numbers are now so old that they are of almost no use to the business owner in his daily management activities. The business owner has paid his accountant for the privilege of informing HMRC how much tax has be to paid.

What a shocking waste. Why not produce accurate numbers throughout the year and use them to better manage the business?

It is also important that the cost and the ease of producing your key numbers keeps pace with the complexity and growth of your business. Never try to grow your business while still running your business using simple spreadsheets.

There are many off-the-shelf financial packages on the market which any bookkeeper or accountant can use to pull your numbers together into a coherent and meaningful system.

Maintaining the integrity and usefulness of your numbers then only requires someone to correctly input ongoing information and ensure that the numbers remain optimum for managing and controlling the business.

Maintaining, monitoring and improving the usefulness of your numbers should become a fundamental habit and attitude within your business. Achieve this habit and your experience as a business owner manager will be enriched in ways you may now only imagine.

Financial strategy challenge two: Overcome your numerophobia

Financial checklist	Doing this!	Do more!	Start doing!
1: Don't avoid the numbers			
2: Put your school view of numbers behind you			
3: Know what financial questions to ask			
4: Find easier ways to understand the numbers			
5: Manage your money			
6: Look for financial improvements			
7: Keep on top of your numbers			
TOTAL			

Transfer your totals to the table on Page 312

Financial strategy challenge three: How do I generate more cash?

Maintaining cash-flow, matching the money coming in with the money going out, is one of the biggest issues for any businesses.

Now, the obvious way to get more cash into the system is to increase sales. But this not only produces cash-flow, it also tends to require more cash-flow, because of the cash required to make additional sales and the time it takes to get paid for these.

All the cash in your business is in one of six places:

Debtors: Cash you have invoiced and are waiting to be paid.

Creditors: Cash you owe out to all your suppliers.

Assets: These may be expensive fixed assets such as machinery, plant, and premises etc. They may also be assets you must have, to carry out your business such as vehicles, specialist equipment etc.

Stock: This may be in the form of physical stock to sell to your customers, or this may be cash tied up as Work-In-Progress – see below.

Business cash at your bank: In your business bank accounts, reserves, etc. This includes cash that you have borrowed from lenders/investors etc. to use in your business.

Shareholders/business owners' cash: Cash that the shareholders/ business owners have withdrawn from their business and are personally holding outside of their business.

The trick here is to understand how to manipulate the above to maximise the cash in your business. This is because, all things being equal:

"The more cash you have access to – the more cash you can make."

Here are 7 things to try. Give all of them a go and choose the ones that work best for you.

1. Deal with debtors

Your debtor cash works in a very simple sequence:

A. You do the work/supply the product/service etc.
B. You deliver and invoice your customer.
C. They pay you.

The idea is to compress this sequence, thus increasing the rate of flow through this sequence. Do the work faster to get paid quicker. Increase the amount of flow through the sequence by increasing your sales to existing and/or new customers.

Of course, if you can get paid in advance of doing the work, then you have the best model possible.

However, when it comes to debtors, it is imperative that you are proactive rather than reactive. Never wait until your clients decide to pay you. Instead, adopt the attitude the you will not tolerate late payments, with the objective of having zero debtors outside of your normal payment terms.

This attitude is created right at the start of your sales process with your Terms and Conditions. These must clearly state your payment terms, and it is wise to draw these to the attention of your customers as you take their order, and obtain clear agreement to them right there and then.

Note that every £ that you are waiting to be paid relates to work you have done, so far without benefit. You have spent cash in your business and passed this benefit onto your creditor and it does not pass back until they have paid you.

It is vital that you focus not only on doing the work for your customers, but also on getting paid for your work.

On the one hand, incentives for early payment can be effective. On the other, penalise bad payers. Don't be afraid to use debt collectors, especially if you are happy to sack the client.

When my clients have problems with debtors, the first job I ask them to do is to write down their 'Cash flow process'.

This will include some or all of the following steps:

- Agree the sale, contract and delivery with the customer.
- Produce and deliver your product/service to your customer.
- Send your invoice.

What you then do is critical to your cash-flow. Do you sit back and wait to be paid? Or do you follow a process? Such as:

A. Check your client has received your invoice and agrees with the amount and the payment date.

B. Check with them when you can expect their payment. Make this as specific as possible. Not "next month", but what day next month?

C. Send them a note or call them a couple of days before payment is due to make sure there is nothing holding up their payment. Check they have all the paperwork and are satisfied with what you have delivered etc.

D. Telephone again on the expected day of payment to ensure that there are no issues.

Having three or four touches with your clients before their payment is due ensures that they don't have many excuses left. Keep it nice and polite, but be consistent.

Many years ago, I was complaining about my clients paying me late to someone who had been successful in business over many years. He told me something I've never forgotten: "Managing debtors to get paid faster is an attitude. Your business must adopt an attitude to being paid on time."

He explained that this attitude is not only to be expected from your financial and accounts staff, but also from your sales staff (especially) and everyone else in your business.

You have not made any profit until you have been paid.

2. Manage your suppliers

Many businesses do not ever consider their suppliers as being an important source of cash-flow. And so they overlook what can be a key area for improvement.

A good starting point here is to write down your 'Supplier process'. This will include some or all of the following steps:

A. Decide which supplier to use.
B. Decide what to buy and place your order with them.
C. Receive and check their delivery to you.

D. Receive their invoice and check it is OK.
E. Pay them when their invoice is due.

When deciding which supplier to use, quality and trust are valuable commodities. The products and services you buy speak volumes to your staff and your clients, so make sure that your supplies are telling the story that you want to tell about your business.

How you deal with your suppliers also tells a story about your business. If you deal shabbily with your suppliers, do not delude yourself that this will not eventually affect your business, as they take liberties with you and word gets out to other suppliers about your behaviour.

Your suppliers are an important source of added value to your business. Their goodwill towards you is a bankable commodity. Treat them well and they will add to your cash-flow. Treat them badly and eventually they will destroy your business.

Thus, it is not advisable to buy on price. But also, never feel obliged to stick to the same supplier just for the sake of it. Look for additional cash-flow and value in your relationships with all your suppliers. This is not just about asking for cheaper prices.

Examine your supplier process for ways to achieve improved cash-flow and profitability (which eventually feeds through into cash-flow). For example, you may persuade your supplier to hold stock for you, so you do not have to pay for it until it is delivered and invoiced to you.

If you have a seasonal business and currently enjoying good cash-flow, perhaps share this with your suppliers and reduce your costs by requesting discounts for early payment, buying increased volumes etc.

You may negotiate increased payment terms. Note the word "negotiate". This does not mean delay without permission. Think of the story you are telling to your staff and your suppliers.

Your business will be some sort of middleman between your suppliers and your customers. Sometimes it is possible to work with key suppliers and customers to increase the sales through your business, and your cash-flow.

Think of the retail sector at Christmas. They negotiate deals with their suppliers to keep their shelves full, up to and over the break. Thus, they sell more and so do their suppliers.

Whatever your business, lots of your cash-flow will go to your suppliers. Aim to derive the maximum benefit to your business for this cash-flow. There will be potential here, but you can't exploit this if you don't put effort into finding it.

3. Reduce your stockholding

If you are in a business that holds stock, you are investing your precious cash-flow into an asset that will hopefully produce a greater cash-flow back into your business.

The trick to managing stock is to keep it moving. This produces cash-flow and stops your cash-flow being tied up for long periods in slow moving stock or, even worse, dead stock that doesn't move at all.

The more that moving your stock is a critical factor to the livelihood of your business, the more important it is to ensure that you know your stock numbers.

Put as simply as possible you have three types of stock:

1) Moving: This is producing the cash-flow you expected when you bought it.

2) Slow-moving: This is not producing your expected cash-flow.

3) Dead: This is not producing any cash-flow.

Once you categorise every stock item into one these three types, then you can take action.

Moving stock

Can you create more cash-flow (and profits) from moving more of this, by using volume discounts, pricing strategies, bundling various items together and so on?

As discussed above, can you do any deals with your suppliers of this stock to maximise cash-flow and profits?

Slow-moving stock

The key here is to create a strategy to move this faster. Again, you can use volume discounts, pricing strategies, and bundling etc. You may bundle with other slow moving items, but a useful strategy can be to bundle with faster moving items. And where possible, with dead-stock items.

This can be an area where having a good relationship with your suppliers can help. You may have several customers for that slow-moving stock item, but your supplier may have hundreds.

It is often worthwhile to ask them to take the stock back, credit you for it and then they sell it to their other clients.

Dead stock

This will cripple your cash-flow if you do not move it. Use every strategy outlined above for recovering cash-flow from slow-moving stock. Additionally, you can note those customers for which you originally bought this stock and do some kind of deal with them to convert your dead stock into cash. Where your dead stock has a shelf-life the challenge of moving it becomes even more urgent.

Earlier I mentioned the importance of having a strong attitude to being paid on time. Stock also requires an attitude, and that is to keep it moving and keep it producing cash-flow.

Sometimes you need to let go, to forget the profit you expected from buying the stock, and just get the stock converted to as much cash as you can.

Businesses that provide services often do not consider that they too have stock. Their stock is Work-In-Progress.

The website half completed and awaiting input from their client. The architectural project waiting to be finalised by the client who is now dragging their heels. Any project where the client is haggling over details such that you have not been able to send your final invoice.

It is useful for these businesses to continually monitor their Work-In-Progress. Which projects have not yet been finally invoiced and why. What are these projects waiting for and can they be moved along?

Again, a focused attitude helps here. And this attitude should be fed by knowing that you have spent your money on creating the outcome for your client. Now it is your turn to be paid for expending your resources to create this outcome.

Understand that not only have you expended your resources to produce the outcome for your client, but also you are continually expending resources and energy to push your client to agree completion of the project.

To maximise your cash-flow in this type of business, you must have terms and conditions of sale and provision that create the attitude where your project work flows through in the minimum time and with the minimum effort to where you can invoice and get paid.

4. Sell unwanted assets

Many businesses have unwanted items of machinery, furniture or even vehicles lying around doing nothing. Not only do these tie up cash, they also have a cost by cluttering up your workspace and your thinking.

Look around your premises and workspaces. Is there anything that you do not use or need? How much cash could these generate if you sold them? Then have a policy of reducing clutter by getting rid of these. Often this may not generate much actual cash, but it all helps, it is an easy win, and there are other intangible benefits to be had from a general reduction in clutter.

Think of other assets owned by your business that tie up cash and other resources. Do you use all the space that your business pays for? Could you reduce this cost and free up cash-flow by reducing the space that you use? Maybe by renting some of your space off to another company?

Then there are more intangible assets within your business that you may consider selling. You may be able to sell more than you can deliver. So, is it possible that you could sell some of this sales capacity to another business to generate more cash-flow?

Similarly, can you produce and deliver more capacity that you can now sell. Could you sell this extra delivery capacity?

The key here is to look at exactly where your cash-flow is being tied up and used. Then investigate whether this cash-flow can be reduced in any way or used more effectively to produce more cash-flow (and profit) than now.

Making your assets work better for your business is a key area for improvement in many businesses. It is always worth the time to make sure that you are making the most from yours.

5. Raise prices

Probably the fastest way to increase income is not by increasing sales, but by increasing prices. Although my experiences with business owner managers tells me that often they find this far from easy.

They may not usually want to to admit it, but most of the screams of protest about increasing prices usually come from within their heads rather than from their customers.

In his informative book, *No B.S. Price Strategy*, Dan Kennedy explains this rather well and I'll paraphrase him here:

> "There are two chains that bind a product to price...One is in the customer's mind, the other is in yours. BOTH must be cut. It's a near certainty that the chain in your mind is bigger, thicker, stronger than the one in the customer's mind. Customers embrace de-linking product and price routinely given reasons to do so. Business owners and salespeople are, ironically, more committed to this linkage."

"Yes," my clients say, "I want (and usually also need) to increase my prices. How can I do that? What if they stop giving me their business?"

"Well," I say, "you must develop a better pricing strategy."

And here are some of the strategies we then go on to discuss:
For new customers or new products:

- Your first priority in increasing your prices is to make sure that all new customers and their prices are at the new level.
- And, of course, when you sell new products to existing customers, make sure that these products are priced at your new level.

For existing customers:

Look first for those customers who you know are getting a good deal from you. Which ones give you the most trouble? Which ones do you have to chase for payment, and who always haggles on price? These are probably customers that you are better off without, so start here by increasing your prices.

You will probably find that some of these customers will accept your new prices and some will not. Either way you have benefitted. You've managed to get paid more for what you do, and/ or you have freed up some of your capacity to get better customers.

Next, turn your attention to all your current customers. Consider every client in terms of the prices they pay and what it really costs you to service them. To take out any personal or other biases it is best to use actual numbers to do this. Increase your prices to these customers, starting first with the least profitable and then working up to your most profitable.

Where possible it is better to gradually increase your prices in small amounts. These prove less noticeable to your clients and easier for you to justify when they spot the changes.

Make a firm decision to increase all your prices to current customers by x% over y time period. Say by 10% over 6 months. Earlier I mentioned attitude and pricing also requires an attitude. Your objective here is to get paid more for doing the same work to produce more cash-flow and more profit.

The main fear with most business owner managers is around what they say when a client spots the increase and asks them to justify it. The way to deal with this is to have your reply ready and be able to say it without any hesitation. And then have the rest of the conversation from the point of view that the increase is a done deal, and just needs to be explained in the right terms and language for that client.

Overcoming mindset issues around your pricing is often the major challenge. You are fighting your beliefs and these can be highly resistant to change where pricing is concerned. But think about what Dan Kennedy says about the "chains of price". If that resonates with you, buy his book. It would prove an excellent investment in your quest to obtain better prices from your clients.

If you want to get rich from your business, you must get your pricing right to maximise your cash-flow (and profits). This is a key area to focus on and will repay your efforts many times over.

6. Find production efficiencies

Any business exists to produce an outcome for its clients and for its owners. Each business is a production process, from the business strategy through marketing and sales to delivering the sold promise to clients. Then getting paid by the clients.

Other parts to this production process include investment decisions in people, plant, and every other asset bought and used by the business.

Thus, there are many areas in which to find production efficiencies. Every way that you can discover and implement how to get more done with less cost, the more profit (and cash-flow) you will produce.

Your work here starts with mapping out each critical stage of your outcome-producing process from beginning to end. Then focus on those stages where you feel you can achieve the greatest improvement. Identify changes to implement and then take action.

This outcome-improving process is never completed. As the business changes and your market proceeds through the phases which all markets follow, then your job as a business owner manager is to continue to look for innovations to reduce costs and increase cash-flow and profits.

Look at who is doing what. Ask why things are being done that way. Adapt and change procedures to increase efficiencies and add value to the outcomes that you produce.

Monitor yourself and your staff. Is the right person doing the right job? The job to which their abilities are best suited? Could any job be given to someone else who will do it more efficiently?

Are the right job and role functions grouped together? Does this or that actual operation fit in that place, with that process, with that role, with that person?

The nature of business is that there is always something you can improve. But take care to start with those areas you know are the costliest, give you the most problems and challenges or create stress for your customers and/or staff.

You are looking to produce the same or better outcomes from the same or reduced cost. Seek to reduce or eliminate any resistance within your outcome-delivery process. Where things are sticking – start there.

Never stop and never give up doing this, as there is much to be gained and you will find new ways to ensure the greater satisfaction of your clients, yourself and your staff, and this will increase the prosperity of your business.

7. Source external money

The last port of call when it comes to generating cash is to obtain it from third party funders.

Before deciding on external funding, firstly make sure that you are already using the funds already available in your business to produce the best outcomes. These are your cheapest funds.

The next cheapest funds are your personal funds and those of your other shareholders. When you approach external funders, you will be asked what additional funding you can insert into the business, so you may as well look at this from the outset.

Bank medium-term funding is the next cheapest and is attractive because the bank puts their money in, you use it in your business and then you pay this lending back over a fixed period. You do not have to give up equity, although in today's financial climate you may have to provide a personal guarantee to repay the loan in the event that the business cannot.

Moving on from these, there are a broad variety of funding methods which are either more or less applicable to your particular situation.

Every source of funds will always require details on exactly what you will use their money for, and will have in mind their risk of loss when lending it to you. This risk will reflect in the return which they expect on their money.

You will already be aware of the main types of funding: bank loans; invoice financing and asset financing. However, there are an ever-increasing range of variations in these products, including financing of individual invoices without having a full facility.

If you need to import stock, you can fund this. If you need to invest heavily in plant or equipment, you can fund this. In fact, you can use any asset in your business as collateral for attracting external funds. When you utilise invoice financing you are borrowing against invoices that your customers owe to you.

It should go without saying that borrowing money must not be undertaken lightly. If you do not have a sound plan to produce a return on the money which pays back the lender and at the same time produces a clear premium for your business, then it is probably time to rethink your business strategy.

When borrowing, you are earning money for someone else.

Nowadays you will also probably be undertaking a personal financial commitment for any borrowing you make on behalf of your business. However, there are times when any business requires additional funds to leverage the opportunity to produce growth, predictability and stability. And on these occasions borrowing can be a real opportunity to create lasting business improvement.

I recommend that business owners speak with a selection of funders before settling on any one method of funding their business. Sometimes government backed grants and subsidised funding schemes are available. These are often not well publicised, but if they fit your specific purposes and types of business, they are very lucrative. There is always someone, somewhere who knows how to find and access these schemes.

Information on specific regional economic development schemes is usually available from the regional council organisations to whom you pay your business rates, and this can be a good starting point. Regional councils have a vested interest in increasing the success of businesses in their areas because more profit equals more jobs, more stability, and more income for them.

You may start with a check on what your regional council is doing and then move onto a more structured discussion with your accountant and bank manager. These will cover the basic methods of funding and you may get suggestions about innovative or subsidised funds that are available to suit your circumstances.

It is not advisable to wait until your situation is desperate. This is no place to start for obtaining the cheapest and most appropriate cash. Give yourself time to do the research; it costs nothing to ask your friends, customers, suppliers and business contacts. They may just have a nugget for you.

Make your borrowing a part of your strategic business plan. Money is an asset in your business, you must sweat it just like any other asset. You must have a definite plan how the incoming cash will create a better business for you.

Do take care to manage your personal risk. If you have the option then always avoid giving a personal guarantee for your business funding. And if you must, take care to limit this as much as you are allowed within the terms of your funding.

Where you require large amounts of cash, then almost definitely you will need to take specialist advice. This may require a basket of funders including banks, specialist venture finance partners, and perhaps, individual private investors (business angels).

These basket-funding options will involve specialists who will help you prepare your business strategy and help you pitch to your potential investors. These specialists will also help you to access all relevant government backed grants and any other funding deals that your business could attract.

Financing and re-financing your business is not a decision to be taken lightly. Its connotations will impact your business and your lifestyle for years to come. Do not (ever) go gently into this, and never without having your ducks in a proper row.

Financial strategy challenge three: How do I generate more cash?

Financial checklist	Doing this!	Do more!	Start doing!
1: Deal with debtors			
2: Manage your suppliers			
3: Reduce your stockholding			
4: Sell unwanted assets			
5: Raise prices			
6: Find production efficiencies			
7: Source external money			
TOTAL			

Transfer your totals to the table on Page 312

Financial strategy challenge four: How can I use the numbers?

Identifying and using the right business numbers is a source of great potential for improving your business, managing your resources more effectively, and providing the lifestyle that you expect as a business owner.

Now, as a business owner manager the following questions will probably spring to mind: What are the numbers I require? How do I get these? Why do I need them? How can I understand them? And how do I use them to best effect?

Of course, your bookkeeper or accountant will play a key role in answering all your questions. But it's your job to find the questions to fuel your discussions with them.

As in all your dealings with professional helpers and advisors, the quality of your questions will determine the quality of service which they will provide. This is because most professionals are set up to provide a reactive approach which always tends to put a limit on their usefulness.

Your questions and the subsequent dialogue allow you to create a more proactive approach, and this will dramatically increase your return from any investments you make in any professional advisor.

A point worthy of mention here is don't go to town spending lots of your cash on producing entirely accurate numbers. They need only be accurate enough for you make effective decisions. As a general rule: Your cost to get 90% accurate numbers will be about 10% of what it would cost you to get 100% accurate numbers.

Here are 7 things to try out. Give all of them a go and choose the ones that work best for you.

1. Work out your client profitability

You spend money to sell to your clients (client acquisition cost) and you spend money to deliver (delivery cost) whatever promise you have sold to them. And you may also incur cost to persuade them to pay you when they have agreed that they will (money collection cost).

In fact, you spend money in every interaction with your clients, from before they become prospects right through to them being regular purchasers of your products or services.

The trick here is to know how much you are spending. Because when you measure that, you can manage it.

When everything that you spend is deducted from the price your customer pays, what remains is your profit. And your profit is the reason why you are dealing with that customer.

By knowing the true costs of dealing with our clients, we know how valuable each customer is to us. It then makes sense to adopt a marketing and sales strategy to attract and sell to more of the most profitable types of customer.

Measuring, rather than guessing, takes the emotion out of the equation. The profitability of our clients is thus not what we *think* it is. It is what we *know* it is. Numbers have no emotion, no opinions and they do not take sides.

The trick is collect ALL the costs throughout the entire process of client acquisition, delivery and money collection for each client or type of client. You will not likely get a completely accurate total cost. But you will produce some useful information to make more informed decisions. And chances are, you will get some surprises.

Do ask your bookkeeper and/or accountant for help with this exercise. They will probably save you lots of time and trouble plus present you with information that is as accurate as possible.

Knowing your client profitability tells you many things including:

- Which customers you want more of
- Which customers you want fewer of
- Those customers you should not be dealing with

Additionally, this cost information tells you what prices you must increase to recover your true costs and make a real profit.

And when you combine this cost information with the detail of your processes surrounding selling, delivery and collection you will also get guidance on which of your processes are the most expensive and thus create a focus for your management attention.

This exercise is not just about discovering which customers you can fleece with increased prices. It is also the start of your work to look objectively at where you add value to your customers, and what it costs you to do this versus the price that they pay.

Then you can improve your products and the processes through which you add and deliver value to your customers, with the objective to increase your prices more than the improvements have cost you, thus increasing your profits.

2. Know your client acquisition cost

Some clients cost more to acquire than others. This may be due to just one or a combination of factors.

Some clients may require a bigger marketing spend to attract. You may currently be marketing via an expensive media because that is currently your only cost effective way of reaching those clients with your marketing message.

For example, if you are some kind of consultant, you may be reaching some of your clients through specialist networking events. And you will need to do this until you can find a cheaper route to attracting your prospects.

Having attracted prospects to your business, you then need to sell them into becoming your clients. And this will cost you money, time and other resources.

When you can allocate a specific marketing and sales cost to any client or group of clients, then do so, as this helps you to be clear on your client acquisition costs for those clients.

Where you have general marketing and sales costs that you cannot allocate to individual clients or client groups, then you must decide how you will apportion these costs to arrive at a representative marketing and sales cost for each individual client or client group.

Allocating all marketing and sales costs provides useful information for you to better target your existing marketing and sales resources, to create additional profits. You also know where to spend more on marketing and sales to generate extra sales.

And also, you know which prospects are most expensive to find and convert into clients. Thus, you can decide how worthwhile it would be for you to reduce your dependence on these clients. You can then make decisions on why you should free up the resources you expend to gain these clients and where to target these resources to gain the most profitable clients.

3. Work out your product profitability

Similar to knowing your client acquisition cost, it is also beneficial to know how much your product or service costs for you to deliver.

Then, for each product or service, you can add your acquisition costs to your delivery costs and compare this to your price. And thus, calculate the profitability of each product or service that you sell and deliver.

Your prices are shown on each invoice to each customer. The challenge here is to dig and dig until you arrive at your total cost for selling and delivering each product or service.

You will usually have some easily identifiable inputs to this cost. For example, if you sell cakes you will know the cost of your raw materials. If you are an electrical installer you will have the components that you buy and then install. If you provide a service such as consultancy, you will know the time that you spend with your clients on the work that you do for them.

For most types of businesses, you will also have other expenses such as general overheads of heat, light, etc. You will also need to have some means to allocate general costs such as admin, bookkeeping, etc. to each product.

The usefulness of information on your product profitability is only as good as how accurate you allocate all your costs to each product or service. Judgement and assumptions always play a part in this. But be as fair and accurate as possible. If product "X" deserves to have more costs allocated to it than product "Y" then make it so. Otherwise your process lacks integrity.

Do make sure that every cost in your business is allocated to every product or service that you provide to clients. This may give you some surprises because you may find, for example, that what you think of as your main earner may not turn out to be as profitable as you have been assuming.

An example of this could be physical delivery costs. Just suppose that you take on urgent work for some clients and this is so urgent that it needs to be delivered by a special (more expensive) delivery method. You must allocate this extra cost to that product and customer rather than lumping it in with your general delivery overhead. Because this extra cost will reduce your profitability of that specific product and customer.

Knowing how much you make from the things that you sell puts you in a powerful position. Understanding what products or services make you the most money tells you where to focus your management effort to increase profits.

Focus your marketing and sales to sell more of those products that produce high returns. And focus your management attention on increasing the margins on those products or services that produce the lowest returns.

4. Work out the lifetime value of each client

Our customers may buy from us just once. For example, we do not buy many high-priced TVs or Hi-Fi systems twice. When we buy a service such as a new website, that service has an immediate value that may last for some time. But we will not usually re-buy that service very often.

The lifetime monetary value of clients who infrequently buy products or services must exceed what it has cost to acquire and deliver to that client. Otherwise there is no profit in the transaction.

We are not going to sell that product or service to them again for some time. But there may be other connected products or services that perhaps complement our original sale which we subsequently sell to our existing clients. And this increases the lifetime value of that client.

For example, we buy a high-priced TV. Then later we may go back and buy a cinema surround sound system, then a Blu-ray or DVD player. And we may then buy some insurance to cover us for future loss or repairs. And so on.

Of course, the major electrical retailers and many other businesses have studied what their customers buy, and take care to have these products and services available with trained sales staff to promote them. By doing this they boost the lifetime value of their customers.

Do note that your most expensive sale to any of your customers will be the first sale. Once a customer has bought from you, your investment to persuade them to buy again is much less than your initial client acquisition cost. Thus, subsequent sales generate a proportionately higher profit as well as adding to the lifetime value of that customer.

In some businesses, our customers buy from us regularly. There are certain staple products such as food that we buy daily or weekly. And often we will buy these from the same supermarket. Often for many months or years.

In business, there are some staples that we frequently buy, such as printed items. We often buy brochures, direct mail items, leaflets, and other sales and marketing support materials from the same printer for many years.

Every time we buy from a supplier we add to the profit of that supplier and make a contribution to our lifetime value to that supplier.

Knowing which of our customers have a high lifetime value is useful for targeting similar customers with our marketing, sales and other resources. Focusing our resources on these customers gives us the highest return on our investment.

We can also use our lifetime value information to develop our offers to these high value customers, in order to further increase their value to our business.

For some businesses, there is also an important reason why the lifetime value of customers proves really useful. When the business owner knows the average lifetime value of his customer or a customer group, he then knows how much he can invest to get this type of customer to buy from him.

Thus, he may invest more money and resources to convert a customer than he earns from the first (and sometime the second) sale, in order to invest in achieving a higher lifetime value.

This is very smart marketing, that can be highly profitable and also confuses your competitors, so they dare not copy your tactics. And it is made possible by understanding the lifetime value of your customer. Spend time on this – it is a sure winner.

5. Work out your average order value

If you take your total sales and divide this by your number of transactions, then you will obtain your average order value. Having done this, you can then take steps to increase this amount by adding other product and/or service offers to sell them at the same time each client buys from you.

Just suppose that you sell upmarket paint etc. and your customer comes into your shop and buys some emulsion paint. Might he also want some gloss paint? Maybe he'll want brushes, white spirit, brush cleaner, glass paper and many other things?

Now, if you have a pre-printed list of all the related products that he or she may want to buy, then it is easy to run through this list with them. And then it is likely that you will increase the value of your transaction.

And you will probably increase the loyalty of this customer because you have provided a better service by providing a reminder of the other items needed for each painting job.

Knowing and understanding the importance of your average order value can help you to develop some useful tactics to increase your profit per customer, and your overall profit.

Think about what you could offer your clients to persuade them to buy more items and increase the average order value. This could be additional products as in the example above or it could be additional services.

For example, when you buy a car, you need a finance package, a servicing package, an additional warranty, car insurance, breakdown recovery etc.

You may use promotions such as buy one, get half price, as commonly offered by booksellers. Or you may bundle several of your products or services together and sell this at a price well below the sum of the individual prices of the bundled items.

There may be all sorts of ways for you to increase your average order value, and it starts with understanding what yours is and how to calculate it.

Of course, to generate more sales, you will also want to increase your total number of customers. The combination of increasing customer numbers and increasing your average order value can have a powerful effect on your sales growth.

In all this, it's crucial to understand the relevant numbers and how to use them to make informed decisions that produce the expected outcomes.

6. Cost and value your time

To arrive at an approximate cost for your time as a business owner, divide the amount you earn per month by the *actual* number of hours you work.

Note that I write actual hours and not what you guess that you work. This gives you an idea of the current value of your time - be prepared for a surprise!

Knowing your true hourly rate provides some useful information:

A. You can compare this rate with what you would like it to be and set about closing the gap. Consider what you would have to pay someone to replace you - this is the *market rate* for your job. On that basis, it's what your business should pay you now if this was affordable.

B. You can cost all the jobs that you currently do in terms of the number of hours that you spend doing them. From this you can arrive at an approximate total cost to your business for each job. This is useful when you are pricing your products, but even more so when you are pricing services. Make sure that you cost all your time spent on every activity including sales, delivery and collecting your cash.

C. You can also calculate what any of your jobs would cost your business if you were paid the hourly rate that you would like to be paid. And this may highlight gaps in your prices between what you may now be charging and what you really should be charging if your business paid you the market rate for your work.

D. You can write an 80/20 list of jobs that you do. The 20% are the jobs that *only* you can do. The 80% are those jobs that you are now doing, but that other people could be employed to do. Writing this list will get your brain working to prioritise the first jobs from your 80% list that you must give immediately to someone else so that you can do more of those 20% of jobs that only you can do.

All this can have a profound effect on the fortunes of your business. For example, currently you may be distracted and not focused enough on your selling jobs and so sales have been slow to build. By scrutinising your time, you create time to do more of these jobs and sales take off.

Working through these steps you will create a definite incentive for you to change the activities you perform in your business. You must shift your focus away from as many of the 80% jobs that you can and onto spending as much time as possible on the 20% jobs.

By doing more of these 20% jobs you will add serious value (and profit) to your business. And then your business can afford to pay you more per hour. So, the whole process is a virtuous circle.

Eventually you will close the gap between your current hourly rate and the market rate for your job. This is a major milestone for any business owner, because at that point your business can afford to replace you, and if you wish, this will enable you to make some positive lifestyle changes.

7. Know the buying patterns of your clients

Depending upon your type of business, your clients may buy from you once and never come back. They may buy from you several times before they stop buying. Or they may continue to buy from you regularly over many weeks and years.

Whatever your business, knowing the buying patterns of your clients gives you useful information that you can use to improve your marketing, sales and delivery of your products or services.

If your business already follows, or can be made to follow this general sales rule:

"The more they buy, the more they buy"

then you can create a sales bonanza by improving everything that you do to ensure that your customers buy more often. Because then this rule applies: when they buy more, they will buy more.

Of course, to know how to make this work in your business, you must be able to measure how often your clients buy from you, and what they spend on each occasion.

Knowing this, you can then start to modify what you do to encourage them to buy more often and buy more on each occasion. (See No 5 above: "Work out your average order value.")

Alternatively, when you look at your clients buying pattern and see that they buy only once and do not come back, you know that you need to work on finding out why this is so and make changes.

You then make improvements to your product or service. To get quick extra sales you may improve any offers that encourage your clients to buy right now. You may need to make changes to any guarantees or other ways that reduce the buying risk for your clients.

And often the most important improvement may be to the buying experience you provide to your clients.

By studying buying patterns, you take out the guesswork, because you can easily measure the impact which any improvement produces on your sales.

Financial strategy challenge four: How can I use the numbers?

Financial checklist	Doing this!	Do more!	Start doing!
1: Work out your client profitability			
2: Know your client acquisition cost			
3. Work out your product profitability			
4: Work out the lifetime value of each client			
5: Work out your average order value			
6: Cost and value your time			
7: Know the buying patterns of your clients			
TOTAL			

Transfer your totals to the table on Page 312

Financial strategy challenge five: How do I plan for growth?

There is a widely-accepted premise in business: "If you are not growing – you are dying". Now that does not mean to say that your business must always be on a continual growth trajectory, but that to counteract changes in your market and to take opportunities that present themselves over time, sometime or other you will want to grow your business.

Sometimes, you either grow or die because this is what you must do at that time. But more often, growth is a strategic choice and so you have the time to plan properly to make improvements at your pace, and allow yourself the opportunity to try out new tactics and make the inevitable mistakes without harming your business.

Here are 7 things to try out. Give all of them a go and choose the ones that work best for you.

1. Find ways to fund growth

Any increase in business, especially where you must increase the amount of stock that you hold, will require extra funding.

The cheapest money that you have access to is that which you generate internally, from your trading activities.

To maximise these internal funds, as well as to make a financial plan to access most any form of external funding, you will need to understand the dynamics that are going on in your business - the financial impact that comes from growing any one area of your business. And how each area impacts on the others.

To reiterate from Financial Article No 3: How do I generate more cash?

All the cash in your business is in one of six places:

i. Debtors: Cash you have invoiced and are waiting to be paid.
ii. Creditors: Cash you owe to all your suppliers.
iii. Assets: These may be expensive fixed assets such as machinery, plant and premises etc. And they may also be assets you must have to carry out your business such as vehicles, specialist equipment etc.
iv. Stock: May be in the form of physical stock to sell to your customers. Or this may be cash tied up as Work-In-Progress – see below
v. Business cash at your bank: In your business bank accounts, reserves, etc. This includes cash that you have borrowed from lenders/investors etc. to use in your business.
vi. Shareholders/Business owners' cash: That the shareholders/ business owners have withdrawn from the business and are personally holding outside of the business.

The trick here is to understand how to manipulate the above to maximise the cash in your business:

Debtors:
Maximise your cash at your bank by checking this continually to make sure things do not slip. Try to find ways to encourage debtors to pay early. And definitely have the attitude that they will pay on time according to your payment terms

Creditors:
To maximise cash in your business, never pay early unless you have a strategic reason for doing so. In times where your cash-flow is suffering, work with your creditors - don't be afraid to ask them to help by temporarily extending your terms. They need you and you need them, so work out ways that you can co-operate to mutually improve your businesses.

Assets:
These lock up your cash when you need to have the maximum available as fluid working capital to fund the day to day cash-flow needs of your growing business. So, avoid spending large amounts of cash on assets unless absolutely necessary. If there are expensive assets that you must acquire, consider other ways to fund these such as asset finance or asset-backed medium-term bank loans etc. Speak to a finance specialist about these options.

Stock:
Take all necessary steps to keep your stock moving. Dead or slow moving stock ties up your cash. Measure this to keep it moving. If you carry out work for clients that you must fund until they pay you, look for ways to improve your cash-flow from these activities. Phase payments throughout the project, specify the completion date at which point you will submit your final invoice, and adopt an attitude that maximises your cash-flow by chasing progress for each project.

Business cash at your bank:
Take all steps to manage this at all times. Plan ahead, know who you have to pay and by when and also what cash you have due to come in. Your bank has very sophisticated systems that monitor how you conduct your bank account. Do not kid yourself that they do not know. So be fair with your bank - be prepared to discuss your future cash-flow expectations before they occur.

Always avoid going cap-in-hand to your bank. They like to plan for bad times and respect you when you do. From time to time you may agree with your bank to increase or reduce your overdraft, or even to provide some structured medium-term loans to fund your working capital or specific purchases.

Shareholders/Business owners' cash:
This is cash that the shareholders/business owners have withdrawn from the business and are personally holding outside of the business. Or that they have saved up from their earnings over the years. Do not use your own cash unless you have a sound plan and strategy in place to withdraw your cash at a later date.

Be a lender into your business, just like your bank or any other investor. This source of cash can be a useful source of short-term funding because it is quick and easy to access.

Ask your accountant or bookkeeper to explain balance and flow of the cash in your business. If you are planning to set out on a high growth phase, do not go there until you understand how your cash works, and what steps you will take to make sure you can remain in control. Do have a plan for contingencies and rainy days.

2. Use the numbers

Taking the time to develop good financial models and to establish adequate financial reporting is an investment that will pay you handsomely over time.

This information is essential when you go for growth, but does not need to be complex. But it will involve you calculating some simple numbers and making some basic assumptions.

- What will be your sales revenue?
- How much will you spend to produce this?
- How much profit will these activities produce?

I usually suggest to my clients that they talk to their accountant and ask him/her to produce a financial model for their business. One that is accurate enough to allow the accountant to check the impact of your decisions *before* you put them into action.

Your business will have no more than a handful of key business drivers. Do not proceed with growth until you are sure what these are and how they work.

Day-to-day management of your business requires you to focus on these main drivers. You will know that when these drivers are positive, your profitability and cash-flow will be on track.

Take time to understand exactly how your business finances work in part and in whole, before you embark on your growth trajectory. This will keep you informed about what is happening and why. And will ensure that when you have to make a decision, that you have the right information to make an informed choice, rather than guess.

If something goes off plan, do not hesitate to pick up the phone to your accountant and ask them to check your financial model and tell you what you must adjust to bring it back on track.

In this way, your numbers will make sure you are going in the right direction, and act like a compass to keep you pointing in that direction.

3. Focus on profit and cash

Before decimalisation in the UK there was a phrase often used in business: "A fast tanner is better that a slow bob."

In today's terms, I'll use the phrase, "A fast £5 is better than a slow £10."

The reason for this is cash-flow. The benefit to your business of getting fast cash is often far better than getting more cash but slower. Most businesses do not cease trading because their profits are not high enough; they cease trading because they run out of cash and cannot pay their costs and expenses on time.

Of course, you must make a profit, because eventually this feeds through into cash-flow. But at all times you must maintain the balance and flow of your cash.

Another trap to avoid is summed up in the phrase, "Turnover is vanity and profit is sanity." It is essential that you never sacrifice profit to achieve increased turnover. Keep an eye on your margins - what is really left from your prices after you have paid all your costs to satisfy your customers?

Your average margin is a key performance indicator. When this fluctuates, always demand to know exactly why. Then take all steps to put it back on track. This will help you avoid the habits that lead you into the "turnover is vanity" trap.

To plan for sustained growth, have a robust enough number reporting system in place so that you know that your prices are high enough to create enough profit to fund your day-to-day business and contribute to your business growth.

Also, ensure that at all times you understand your cash-flow position. Never take management decisions about money without knowing and considering the impact of that decision. If you don't know, then delay until you do.

And before increasing sales and adding extra turnover, understand the impact of this upon the balance and flow of your cash.

4. Put cash first, recruitment second

There is always a temptation to hire extra staff in order to grow your business. You want to avoid customer complaints, and listen to pleas from your staff that there is too much work to do and not enough people.

There can be no hard and fast rules here. Sometimes it is appropriate to hire first and avoid the problems of understaffing. And sometimes it is beneficial to wait until your system is creaking under real pressure before employing extra staff.

It is a judgment call for you. But you can make it an easier decision by analysing the financial impact of adding more staff before you make the decision.

If you know what financial contribution you should expect from your new staff member, then you know what you can measure them against. Then they will either produce what you expected or they will not. Also, if you notice your new staff member is not getting up to speed, you can take early steps to correct this with better guidance and training, or let them go.

Employees are easily our most expensive asset, but they are also our most productive asset.

As a general rule, I advise my clients to ensure that they are gaining the maximum benefit from their existing team before employing anyone extra. You can start this process by analysing your labour costs and allocating them to your main selling and delivery processes.

Include yourself in this analysis, but bear in mind that as productive as you are, you are not scalable - there is only one of you.

Adding more staff immediately increases your overheads and, depending on how fast your new employee starts to contribute to the profitability of your business, it may be some time before you achieve an adequate return on that extra salary.

Have numbers in place to check whether you make a profit from every one of your employees. This will inform you if things start to slip. Each person you employ must produce enough extra profit for your business to offset the short-term negative cash flow which they cost.

Always focus on deriving the maximum income from your existing labour resources and have the numbers to prove this. Then you will be more confident about adding more employee cost exactly when you need this and not before.

5. Pay yourself a fair (market) wage

Many business owners start in business by paying themselves only what they feel their business can afford at that time. This will usually be far below the fair or market wage the business would have to pay for that worker.

Now, there is nothing wrong with that. So long as this underpaying strategy does as intended - generate cash within the business. The worst crime of all is when it leads to under-pricing and/or over-delivering of your products and services to your clients.

Note: Over-delivering is where you deliver far too much value to your clients in relation to the actual price which they have paid.

As you grow your business, there is only one of you and you have only 40-50 hours per week available to work in the business.

Thus, the ability of your business to pay you the market wage becomes imperative, since you will eventually need to outsource work to extra direct employees or outside suppliers.

If you have been paying yourself well below the fair market wage, then you will not have enough money available within your pricing structure to employ additional help. And your business will be stuck because you are doing too much yourself and there will not be enough money to buy additional help.

If you currently do not value your time appropriately, then get started on this right now. Otherwise you will continue to distort the actual profitability of your business and severely limit your business growth prospects.

Treat yourself just like you would any other employee. You are either making an acceptable profit for your business or you are not. Sooner or later, like any other employee, you will need to be replaced by someone from the labour market.

By paying yourself less than the fair market wage, you cannot be replaced without producing a financial shock to your business. So, if there is a gap between what you pay yourself and what you should pay yourself, calculate this gap and start to close it now by taking all steps to increase the profitability of your business.

6. Know what's in the bank and what's on its way

Whatever your business, you will provide something to your clients. Then you will invoice for that. Then you will get paid by the client.

You can't be paid what you have not invoiced, so make sure that you invoice as soon as you can. This gets the clock ticking. Once you have invoiced, you can estimate when that amount will be coming in from that client.

Over time, you will come to know the payment patterns of each client. From that you can accurately predict when you will receive your outstanding cash.

By keeping a close eye on your bank balance and knowing with some accuracy when your cash will arrive, you can keep tabs on the payments due from each client.

Keeping on top of these numbers informs your credit control procedure. You know when to ask for payments from clients and you know accurately when you can do this. You know when they are late and how late they are.

You cannot pay your wages, suppliers, rent, utilities etc. on time, unless you have enough cash in your bank to settle these. You will probably also have standing orders and direct debits. Knowing how much these are and when they are paid out is useful in monitoring your bank balance.

When you embark on a higher growth strategy, a useful tip is to operate two lists:

- Cash due in
- Cash due out

Then tick the cash movement off as it occurs.

This keeps you in touch with exactly how your cash is flowing. And you know what cash you must get in from every debtor to enable you to settle each outstanding creditor.

When growing your business, cash is a highly valuable resource. If you run out of cash, your growth will stop and you may even put your business into a cash crisis.

But usually, "When you are resourceful, you will not lack resources". So be resourceful by staying on top of your banking and ensure that you receive cash from your clients as quickly as possible.

7. Develop team effort

As the business owner. it is your job to ensure that when you decide it is time to grow your business that you have enough cash available as and when required.

But never forget that this is a team effort. The trick is to involve exactly who needs to be involved and be clear on the extent to which they will be held responsible for their inputs.

It is about communicating the right message and attitude towards cash in your business. There must always be a general understanding of your overall business growth strategy; this can be just the basic, "How much and by when" communication. Or it may be more detailed. A good rule here is to ensure that each person has enough information about what is expected from them and why this is so.

To become committed to your business results, most people like to know why they need to do what they must do. To keep people involved, this must be clear and kept clear at all times.

As your business grows, this will result in inevitable change and some people find this challenging and stressful. Being clear why the business must grow helps people to deal with this change, and also with any general hassles that occur as your business adjusts to a higher scale.

It is your job to keep the business on track, and to have a set of numbers that tells everyone who needs to know, exactly where you are at all times with the business. Keep people updated so they can make their decisions as much as possible in real time, and with all relevant information to hand.

If you ensure that your team understands the big picture, their part in it, and why you need their help, this will help you to deal effectively with setbacks and take maximum advantage of opportunities that arise.

You will then not only have your ideas and solutions, but they will also add theirs. And when you act on their ideas, they will accept accountability for their results.

To maximise your business growth, without taking everything upon yourself, involve your team, get them all on the same page, and watch your business fly.

Financial strategy challenge five: How do I plan for growth?

Financial checklist	Doing this!	Do more!	Start doing!
1: Find ways to fund growth			
2: Use the numbers			
3: Focus on profit and cash			
4: Put cash first, recruitment second			
5: Pay yourself a fair (market) wage			
6: Know what's in the bank and what's on its way			
7: Develop team effort			
TOTAL			

Transfer your totals to the table on Page 312

Financial strategy challenge six: How can I spend my money wisely?

It is the purpose of your business to produce value for its clients and profit for its owners. Your business will have strategic objectives, these may involve shrinking, consolidating or growing.

To carry out whatever strategy you decide to follow, your business will require cash to fund your plans. And it is your job to make sure that enough cash is available as and when it is required.

It is also your job to ensure that this hard-earned cash is spent as wisely as possible to further the business objectives; to produce the highest returns using every resource that is available to you.

Here are 7 things to try out. Give all of them a go and choose the ones that work best for you.

1. Plan your spending

Sometime during your business year, it is advantageous to set time aside to consider your plans for the following year: the next 90 days in detail and the next 9 months in less detail. Include in this an estimate, as accurate as possible of how much cash you will need to fund your annual plan.

Make your overall plan first and then estimate the cash each phase or part of your plan will require.

If you struggle with this, ask your accountant for help. This is also useful as a check of your accuracy, and to make sure that you have considered as many "what ifs" and contingencies as possible.

You do not want to run out of cash halfway through a specific project such as a marketing and sales process aimed at increasing your sales. Do be conservative, and where there are unknowns and guesses involved, it is wise to create a reserve of cash for any emergencies.

By having the discipline to consider your cash requirements, you will be encouraged to create more detail around and within your plans, and this is beneficial to make you think through as many outcomes as possible.

The idea is to think and work through as many outcomes as you can think of and thus take out as much guesswork as possible. Ideally you want cash in place for every outcome that you have considered.

Each project in your plan will have its own cash requirement. Included in this will be a forecast of what you need to start and finish that project. You will then need to add up each amount to create a cash forecast that meets the needs of your overall strategy.

As you progress through the coming year, you can then use this forecast to track your spending on your overall strategy and for each project within it. This will keep you on track and in control of your spending.

2. Know your ROI

Each amount of cash that you spend in your business should be spent to solve a problem for the business. The trick is to define this problem correctly before you spend the cash, and then afterwards you can check if the problem has been solved.

When you can do this, you will always be clear on your Return On Investment (ROI) for all spending in your business. Some of your ROI may be seen immediately. Some may take some time to work through.

You may have some kind of rule or expectation about seeing a total ROI from any spending within a specific time. For example, an often-used rule for spending on a large asset may be a full return of the cash spent within 18 months. Some of this will come back in immediately the asset comes into use, and the rest within the 18 months.

This could be the case for an IT installation to make your business more efficient. Or the purchase of an expensive machine to take out a bottleneck in your production process and increase overall productivity.

The point is that everything you spend your money on should make you money in the long run. It might save you money, time or staff costs. Or improve the quality of your customers' experience in dealing with you. Whatever you spend your cash on, there must be an ultimate benefit to you and your business.

Testing and measuring (T&M) is crucial here. This is all about trying (investing in) new things to create improvements (this is your testing) and then measuring the results to quantify and ensure that the expected improvements are as expected to your ROI.

It is highly beneficial for you to apply T&M techniques to ensure that you maximise your ROI on any spending. And also use T&M to decide where to spend your cash to produce the greatest ROI.

By firstly planning your spending, you'll know why you want to make the investment and the results that you expect from it.

By using T&M to check your ROI from each project that you do, you will dramatically improve your future investment decisions. And this will create a gradual improvement of your ROI from every investment decision that you make.

3. Understand more about your power balance

Essentially, your business sits in your market between your suppliers on one side and your customers on the other. The function of your business is to convert your supplies into something valuable that you can sell to your customers and create the highest benefit or profit for your business.

To maximise the profits of your business it can be useful to consider the power balance between you and your customers. And also between you and your suppliers.

To help you understand your power balance, make a two-column list:

In the left-hand column list, all your suppliers. To ensure that you have included all of them, check your accounts and for every cost, list the supplier you use for every payment that you make.

Create this list in descending order, from highest to lowest expenditure. That's every supplier you pay in order to satisfy your customers. To keep things simple, you may wish to group some of these suppliers together.

It's useful in this exercise to allocate specific suppliers to specific customers or customer groups, if that is possible. However, some suppliers will be providing items or services that are applicable across your entire customer base.

In the right-hand column list your all customers. Again, create this list in descending order, from highest to lowest importance customers to your business.

If there are not many customers, list them individually. If there are a large number of customers, list them as customer segments. Segments may be by products or services sold, or by size. It is also useful here to segment this customer list by profitability.

By doing this you will begin to get a feel for the relationship that your business has with each supplier and customer. And then you are able to focus on the key ones to better serve your business.

You now know where these key relationships are and can look for opportunities to adjust the power balance between them and your business.

All your suppliers (don't forget you and your staff here) depend upon your business to provide them with earnings. And this process will highlight where adjusting the power balance will directly benefit your business.

You may discover opportunities to reduce costs or increase prices, or just receive better value for your money. And these changes will feed through into extra profits.

Similarly, with your customers, there will usually be some of these where you must or could adjust the power balance. You may increase your prices or instigate reductions in whatever you supply to them. And this will increase your profits.

By working out where you are in relation to every supplier and customer, you can create a hit-list of where to adjust the power balance in favour of your business.

One thing is for sure in business and in life generally: "If you don't ask, you don't get." The key here is to target those who do not give your business the best deal that you should expect, or that you already achieve from other suppliers and customers.

You always have the power to ask. And your suppliers and customers can always say "No". But for every one that says "Yes" you make an immediate gain. So, make a list to target and get working to adjust your power balances to increase your profits.

4. Evaluate risk v reward

If being in business was a sure bet, then every business owner would be wealthy and live the perfect lifestyle. But there are no such certainties in business.

Every business exists within the whole market. Each business creates its window of opportunity in its market and this can open and close totally independently of anything which the business owner can influence.

There is an unpredictability in business and this creates a risk that we must attempt to manage every day. We can plan our investment in our business, and forecast an ROI, but there can be no guarantee that this will work out as planned.

Some of us have a low tolerance to risk; we are risk averse. And we are prepared to accept a low ROI provided that our investment in this is low risk. Others are more prepared to embark on a higher risk strategy that could produce a potentially higher reward. We each have our own personal relationship with risk.

Also, some strategies will be potentially riskier than others. There may be more unknowns and we may have to make more assumptions about their inputs and outputs. There may be gaps in our knowledge about the strategies and tactics we are proposing. And we may not be sure if the market will work for or against us.

It is essential for you to be clear about your attitude to business risk and to factor this into your strategies and plans. You may be more risk averse because you feel that you lack some key knowledge, but you may undertake the investment anyway because the only way to obtain this knowledge is to carry through with your strategy. Or you may delay this investment until you have gained that knowledge.

Some strategies may carry too much risk for you and so you scale back the project in order to test the strategy in a less risky way.

It is important for the prosperity of your business that you are comfortable in evaluating each risk before embarking on a particular investment. Then you can change your tactics to modify each risk until it becomes acceptable to you.

These are some of the ways that you can manage and reduce your risks, while at the same time maximising your rewards. It pays to be sure of exactly what you are committing, and what you are prepared to lose.

5. Spread your payments around

There will probably be times in your business when there is just not enough cash to pay everyone who is due for payment. And you may have to spread your available cash to satisfy as many creditors as possible.

If you get into this position, know exactly where you are: what cash is due from your debtors and what is due to your creditors, and when these funds are expected to go out and come in.

Then you can see the whole picture and decide on your tactics. Of course, push your debtors to pay you as soon as possible. And work with your creditors by telling them how you will deal with their outstanding payments, instead of leaving it until they come to you.

You may be surprised how quickly word spreads among your suppliers when one of their customers starts to pay late. Don't let them be talking about you. Get in first with a payment plan for them. Tell them what you will pay and when you plan to pay it. Then do all that you can to make this happen.

For any supplier, receiving some money is better than no money. Just as talking to them is better than ignoring their requests for payment. You are also a supplier to your customers, so treat your suppliers how you would like your customers to treat you if they were late in paying you.

Avoid paying one creditor the total amount that they are owed and then paying nothing to the others, even if there may be strong pressure for you to do this, such as they may have refused to supply you unless you pay up. Be prepared to negotiate, even with these hard suppliers. They will listen if your story is persuasive enough. But be certain that you can pay what has been promised and by the date specified. Otherwise, you place yourself in an even worse position, having created an additional breach of trust.

However, if you have made promises to your suppliers which you then keep, they will be more inclined to help you out the next time around.

Always be prepared to negotiate payments with your suppliers. Keep communication open with them throughout any difficulties that you have. And don't forget to thank them for their help and patience once you are through and out the other side.

6. Define as costs or investments

You will be spending your cash to generate sales. And to deliver whatever promise you have sold to your customers. As a general rule, any cash that you spend that provides a clearly identified cash return you can class as an investment.

For example, you will be spending money on sales and marketing activity and this will be generating sales revenue. There may be a direct relationship between this spending and sales revenue, so that doubling the spending produces double the sales revenue.

Or it may be that when you consider individual sales and marketing activities, some of your investments in these produce measurable increases in sales revenue, but some do not.

A useful distinction is that those that produce a measurable return are *investments* and the rest are classed as *costs.*

It is thus useful to check everything that you are currently spending your money on to generate sales and to check whether each of these are producing an acceptable return on your invested cash.

Do note here that you may also be investing your time or other resources, so decide your cost for these and factor these into your calculations. When you do this across all your sales and marketing activities be prepared for some surprises!

Look at every activity, starting first with those that you spend most resources on. Reduce or eliminate those activities that are not producing an acceptable return.

Check expenditure on advertising; website activities such as SEO and Google AdWords; all your networking activities; email and direct mail marketing; telesales; your sales force costs; your use of printed materials, brochures and all other sales tools; everything that draws on your company's resources.

Next, look at every other major cost showing in your business accounts. These may just be standard costs associated with being in business such as payroll, administration, utilities, telecoms, business rates, bookkeeping, HMRC employment costs etc.

Then ask yourself whether any of these costs are excessive and could be reduced. Be prepared to get a second opinion from an outsider who has experience in other businesses, such as your bookkeeper or accountant.

Start with you highest expenditure and then work down your list. Check each item of expenditure in this way, and keep asking whether it could be reduced. Note that any expenditure reductions will convert directly into extra profit.

Or you could invest these savings into other areas that you have discovered will produce a better ROI, such as a direct increase in revenue and profit.

It is your job to balance all your expenditure (investments and costs) to produce the biggest overall return (profit) from your business.

Don't forget that there are some expenditures that you must make without any guarantee of any return.

Examples of these are innovation expenses. Occasionally you will need to allocate cash and other resources to try out new ideas and ways to sell and deliver your products or services.

Sometimes these will lead to an overall improvement in your profits and other times you will not see a tangible return. But in all cases such innovation always leads to an increase in your knowledge about your business.

Sometimes you have to pay in order to learn what to do and what not to do - there is no other way.

7. Decide on the present, not the future

For major expenditure items, it is recommended that you do not make any investment in these unless you have the full amount sitting ready in your business cash reserves.

To avoid putting your business at risk, and you under pressure, never make these investments based on cash that you have yet to earn from future sales or other revenues.

You must work with the cash that you know you have, not what you think you will have.

In the event that you have no choice but to make a large investment without having the cash already in your reserves, investigate other ways to pay for the investment.

If it is an asset, then look at asset finance. If your investment is less tangible, then ask your bank for an increase in your overdraft, or for a medium-term loan.

Get resourceful when looking for ways to finance major expenditure. Offers of business funding are constantly changing and evolving.
If you are in a business which will eventually require outside funding, it is wise to keep in touch with the finance market so that you know who to speak with if you need to borrow.

Never put yourself in any situation where you are leaving things to chance. Because when it can go wrong, then it may.

'Murphy's Law' will occur if you provide the opportunity through poor cash planning.

You may find that a large customer, who is your best friend and who would never buy elsewhere, finds a better deal, suddenly does not buy so much, and then switches to your competitor. Or the large invoice you have outstanding will not now be paid because that customer has filed for insolvency.

For information, Murphy's Law is:

Nothing is as easy as it looks
Everything takes longer than you expect
Anything that can go wrong – does go wrong...
And at the worst possible moment

Financial strategy challenge six: How can I spend my money wisely?

Financial checklist	Doing this!	Do more!	Start doing!
1: Plan your spending			
2: Know your ROI			
3: Understand more about your power balance			
4: Evaluate risk v reward			
5: Spread your payments around			
6: Define as costs or investments			
7: Decide on the present not the future			
TOTAL			

Transfer your totals to the table on Page 312

Financial strategy challenge seven: How do I fund a new venture?

As established business owners, sometimes we see an opportunity to invest our time, money and resources more profitably in another venture.

This may be because we do not feel comfortable to continue investing in our current business. Our business growth may have levelled off or even be decreasing.

Our window of opportunity may be shrinking or there may be negative shifts and trends in our current market. We may be experiencing strengthening competition and feel that we do not want to undertake the investment to counter this.

We may have the opportunity to sell our existing business, and decide this is our best option. Or it may be that the new business opportunity is just too lucrative to pass up.

Whatever our reason, there will be a number of things to consider before we start our new venture.

Here are 7 things to try out. Give all of them a go and choose the ones that work best for you.

1. Go with sheep not rabbits

Firstly, make sure that your new venture is not just a distraction. There is a phrase that says, "A dog can only chase one rabbit at once".

This is because when a dog chases two rabbits they head off in different directions and the dog cannot follow both. However, a dog can herd a flock of sheep, because sheep tend to run together.

Give due consideration as to whether your new venture is a 'rabbit' or a 'sheep'.

Do your current and new venture share the same sales and delivery processes? Will you be selling in the same way to the same type of customers? Will your current and proposed processes be similar? Will you use the same suppliers or supplies?

Can your staff cope with the existing and the new business? Will you?

The greater the number of common factors between your current and new venture, the more that the two of them are 'sheep' rather than 'rabbits'.

Where your current and new venture have hardly anything in common, then watch out because they may become 'rabbits' and head off in entirely different directions.

The more that they diverge in different directions, the more difficult you will find managing both businesses at once. Your staff will also suffer distraction as they and all your other business resources become split between the two businesses.

Until ultimately you may be forced to make a choice which 'rabbit' you will chase. And which you will let go.

When my clients start to discuss new ventures with me, I begin by asking them to decide which business they are most passionate about making a success. Which one will be the one that gets them out of bed every day?

Then, unless they can convince me that both businesses are 'sheep', I recommend that they make whatever changes they need to put all their efforts into the one business they are most passionate about, and not the other. And chase only one 'rabbit.'

2. Decide on the legal structure

This is important because it defines how you do everything going forward after you start out.

When you have 100% ownership, you have control of the structure and you can decide more or less what structure you want. It is still wise to talk this through with your accountant to decide which type of company has the best tax structure for your circumstances, and the best opportunity to grow.

With 100% ownership, you basically have two structures. You can have a limited company, which limits your liabilities from your business. Or you can have a proprietorship where you are in law totally liable for most things than can happen with your business.

Alternatively, you can have the new business trading as part of your existing business. This may be OK at the outset but can become complicated, so watch out if you go this route.

Your new business may be a joint venture with someone else. In this case I recommend that you go down the limited company route to protect you from whatever your new partner may get up to. And you must speak to a business formation specialist who will take you through a standard checklist covering your requirements and options.

You must also set up the structure of a limited company to take into account future changes to the business and its directors. For example, how they can sell out their shares or leave the business etc.

Do spend enough time to get these joint venture structures right, not only at the outset, but with the right ongoing structures in place to take account of future challenges and opportunities.

For example, the current directors (including you) may want to sell out and move on. At that point, you may need to attract new directors and shareholders to inject money or specialist skills to enable the business to grow and develop

It really is worth getting the right business structure from the start. You will not want to be held up later, maybe under financial pressure, and be forced into making changes that adapt your business to changed business conditions.

I recommend that you give this matter all due consideration by writing down your thoughts and then checking them with a specialist, before starting your new venture.

Keep it simple and keep it flexible, but make it work for you and not against you.

3. Make sure it's different

If you wish to promote two businesses into the same geographic market, or within the same customer base, you must take care to avoid confusing your prospective clients.

If you have been offering one type of product or service and then you suddenly start promoting another very different product or service, then your prospects are likely to get confused and ask questions such as:
- "Now you are selling this product, are you still offering the previous products?"
- "If we want the previous products, do we still buy these from you in the same way, at the same prices, etc.?"
- "Who do we send our orders to?"

Also, bear in mind that any negative connotations from your earlier offers will impact on your prospects' acceptance of your new offers. Bad news will carry over, but so will good news. Those who have bought successfully in the past are likely to listen sympathetically to your sales pitch for your new business offer.

Make sure there is a clear distinction between your new venture and your existing business. Your new business must add to your standing in the market and not reduce it. If you have a good reputation for supplying good quality offers, make sure that your new offers maintain this reputation.

You will also need to tell a story about why you are offering new products or setting up a new business. Potential clients will want to know your agenda. When they understand why you are doing what you do, they will be more inclined to trust you.

Create clarity and space between your existing and new businesses and their products or services. Be clear about any differences between the existing and new in the ways customers buy from you, the processes by which you deliver your product or service, or any other ways that you can identify.

The more that you can differentiate between the existing and new, the greater will be your opportunity to maximise your overall sales. More clarity and differentiation equals less confusion. And less confusion equals more sales.

You must decide whether your new venture requires its own company structure, branding, sales and marketing, premises, etc. Often it is better to go for a complete separation, to avoid tainting your current business in case your second venture does not work out.

It happens that we often see market opportunities that are not best served through an existing business structure. We decide to set up another business structure to launch our new venture. We may keep the ownership secret or we may use our existing business as a launch-pad.

There are many pros and cons to be considered before we add to the complexity of our lives and businesses. As a rule, only let your choice become as complex as it needs to in order to fulfil the objectives of your new business venture, and no more.

To minimise your distraction when running two business ventures, give lots of due consideration to the sheep and rabbits notes explained in No 1 above.

4. Get the right team

In his excellent book, *From Good to Great*, Jim Collins mentions "Who comes before what" when he talks about the importance of management teams.

Collins states the importance of getting the right team (*who*) in place before you shift the business into a different emphasis (*what*).

There is only one of you and you can't clone yourself, so you must be able to rely on your team. They must be able to manage and grow both businesses with you.

Your team members may be dedicated to either business or they may have roles in both businesses. To decide who will do what, you must again consider rabbits and sheep, to ensure that each team member suffers minimal distraction.

For example, your bookkeeper is unlikely to be too distracted working for two different businesses. But your sales team would probably be highly distracted.

And your marketing team's efforts will probably work best if completely separated.

For each team, it is your job to maximise the focus of each individual and minimise their distraction. Each person must understand what they are accountable for and why, and the results upon which they will be measured and evaluated.

If both your teams are in contact with each other, you must watch out for conflict. This is contagious and will lead to a lack of commitment if you do not correct it.

Your leadership will always make a huge difference to your results, until that leadership is taken up by the right leaders within your team. Your team are there to help you solve the challenges and problems of the business, and to create optimum results from the opportunities that present themselves in your markets.

If you struggle with managing people to their optimum performance, don't believe that *"good leaders are born and not made"*. This is not true. But you must create the environment for your people to grow into effective leaders.

People are your most expensive resource; they are also your most productive. So, if you feel lacking in the skills needed to develop an effective team, consider getting help with your leadership development.

The better that you are at leadership, the better you will generally be at developing leadership within your team.

5. Define roles and responsibilities

When undertaking your new venture, you will probably be the project manager for the new venture, and so start with yourself. Write out your own roles and responsibilities first.

You may write this exactly as it is now, and also your expectation of what it will be at some future time. This future expectation, for now, may just take a simple type of approach, such as, less of this and more of that; stop this and start that. A keep it simple type of approach.

For now, focus on your current roles, because once you have stated these, you then know what you can expect from your other team members. And you can go on to discuss and agree the roles and responsibilities of the rest of your team.

Every job, role and responsibility should be covered. And, something that may easily be missed at the start of this exercise, make sure that each one is given specifically to one person. Some jobs and projects etc. may have a shared workload. Make sure that the responsibility for keeping these shared jobs on track and bringing them in on time rests firmly with one person. This will save you a world of grief, and make you money.

This type of personal responsibility works because you only have one person to speak to about that shared job. He or she is not allowed to lay blame on those who help them with that responsibility if the job does not complete as specified and on time. It is their responsibility to inform you when and if the job is not on track and why. If they take direct responsibility from you, they are focused on the job in hand. And this leaves you to focus on work that requires your particular abilities.

Having agreed who is responsible for what, also ensure that everyone knows how their success and performance will be measured. This further clarifies your expectations.

Any new venture will not only require a large investment in time, energy and money, but also will create distractions in your other business for you and anyone on your team who is involved in both businesses. Minimise this by being very clear about roles and responsibilities, who is doing what, and who is responsible for what. Clarify how each team member's performance will be measured and when results are expected to be delivered.

If you see anyone stalling, lacking clear direction or poorly focused, they are unlikely to turn in their responsibilities on time. Speak to them and find out their problem. Work through their challenges with them until they are back on track. If they aren't able to, you will need to re-allocate their responsibilities around your other team members to maintain momentum.

A final point here is to ensure that your team reports back to you on progress and on hold-ups. Do not slip into the habit of pushing the initiative for communication in the other direction, i.e. you checking in with them. This will destroy your focus on your responsibilities and your time will evaporate.

By all means check in with your team at regular meetings, and/or set up some kind of measuring and reporting system that indicates whether you are on track or not.

With every team member, create the expectation that they are responsible for telling you what is on track, and if it is not on track, then exactly what they are doing to rectify the situation.

Keep in mind that it's your job to help your team *"manage the exception,"* not to help them *"manage the rule"*.

6. Recycle as much as possible

You will have learned lots of do's and don'ts in your current business. You'll know what works well and what doesn't. Take the opportunity to replicate what works and eliminate what does not.

Avoid wasting resources by not reinventing the wheel or reinventing a broken wheel. Also, avoid wastage by not replicating anything in your current business that is not currently running exactly as you want.

Use your previous experience of what works and what does not to start your new venture with a clean sheet. Recycle and re-use what works well, and only transfer systems or processes whose performance you have tried and tested.

Apply the same recycling process to those people who work for you inside your current business. Stop any bad habits or substandard working practices from transferring over into your new business. You have a great reason to do things differently, so use it.

Similarly, with those people who are your suppliers, only carry over the relationships that are currently working for you. Take this opportunity to do things differently and better.

Audit each part of your current business and decide whether you will recycle each element as it is now, or you will modify, or you will find and use a new and different practice.

Take this opportunity to evaluate every area of your business. For example, look at your website; your CRM system; your sales and marketing systems; your products and the systems you use to deliver these; employment policies such as wages, salaries and bonus structures; and your financial systems and practices.

Never carry over anything that does not work to your satisfaction. But save money, time and resources by continuing to do what works and produces the outcomes you want.

7. Only put in what you're prepared to lose

With any new venture, it is really important that it stands on its own feet as quickly as possible.

We have all heard of new ventures which not only never got off the ground, but also pulled down the business owner's existing business. For this reason, it is important to set targets of the "how much and by when" type.

How much cash and resources will you put into the new venture until it stands on its own feet and generates the required return? How much safety margin will you allow if it does not work out as planned?

At what point would you say, "Enough is enough" and it is time to shut down the new venture?

It is important that you never start a new venture that is under-resourced, as this is a sure way to limit your chances of success. Thus, make sure that you consider as many eventualities as possible before hitting the start button.

For example, you will never want to be a situation where you expend all your resources to establish your new business, to the point where your new business struggles because you have not allowed for enough cash to fund your marketing.

Consider as many possible outcomes as possible and have strategies to cover all the eventualities.

Remember Murphy's Law:

Nothing is as easy as it looks
Everything takes longer than you expect
Anything that can go wrong – does go wrong...
And at the worst possible moment

Once you launch the new business, you can't hold back. It will require 100% effort and commitment to get it live, running and stable. But do your homework and be realistic with your "how much and by when's".

Avoid the temptation to get dragged into providing more and more resources into a new venture that is not yet profitable.

It is your risk and it is impossible to prosper as a business owner if you do not innovate, and innovation always has its risks and rewards.

Only you can decide when enough is enough, and how much you are prepared to lose in your new venture.

Be ready to fund the business if things to take off. But if things do not work out as planned, take those hard decisions that must be taken. If you are unsure what to do, then do not hesitate to get expert advice and then act upon this.

Financial strategy challenge seven: How do I fund a new venture?

Financial checklist	Doing this!	Do more!	Start doing!
1: Go with sheep not rabbits			
2: Decide on the legal structure			
3: Make sure it's different			
4: Get the right team			
5: Define roles and responsibilities			
6: Recycle as much as possible			
7: Only put in what you're prepared to lose.			
TOTAL			

Transfer your totals to the table on Page 312

The next steps and action summary

There is a lot of information contained within this book.

Five main areas.

x

Seven categories in each main area.

x

7 action points for each category.

=

That is **245** action points to have a go at.

We don't expect you to do all of them in one go. Your first step is to focus on the area that is most important to you.

As you progressed through the book, you will have completed the tables at the end of each category to find your current position. If you go back and total up the number of ticks in each column, you can get a total score for each table.

Transfer those results into the summary table we've pulled together right after this section.

You can then see, at a glance, which areas you need to be focusing on first.

However, what if the information you are looking for isn't here? Maybe the answers in this book are not relevant to you or you can't see how it will work in your case. Perhaps you're not even sure what the question is that you need an answer to.

Then why not get a direct answer to your specific issue?

Email us on hello@howacademy.co.uk

Send us your question or area of concern, with any background information you feel relevant.

And we will do what we can to get you the answer you need - even if we need to arrange a call to make it happen.

- If you want to make a real change to your business.
- If you have the drive to do what's needed to make that change.
- If you believe that you need to spend some time now in order to benefit in the future.

Then drop us a line.

At most, it'll cost you the price of a phone call.

Otherwise, good luck and we wish you well in your pursuit of a better business.

Action summary

To see the strategy areas you need to be focusing on, look back at the ticks you put in each column in each of the seven checklists in each strategy area. Then tot up the number of ticks you put in each column and translate these into a number in each column here. This will show you at a glance which areas to prioritise.

Personal strategy Seven x7

Seven common challenges in personal strategy

Personal strategy checklist summary	Doing this!	Do more!	Start doing!
1: Enjoy life more			
2: Enjoy my business again			
3: Find time for myself and my family			
4: Improve my relationships			
5: Improve my financial position			
6: Become better at what I do			
7: Improve my health			

Business strategy Seven x7

Seven common challenges in business strategy

Business strategy checklist summary	Doing this!	Do more!	Start doing!
1: Work out where I'm going			
2: Work out who we are			
3: Work out how to stabilise			
4: Make more money			
5: Work out how to grow			
6: Become better at what I do			
7: Develop an exit plan			

Sales strategy Seven x7

Seven common challenges in sales strategy

Sales strategy checklist summary	Doing this!	Do more!	Start doing!
1: Increase profits by selling more			
2: Improve my marketing			
3: Improve my margins and profits			
4: Use marketing to improve margins			
5: Increase profits through positioning			
6: Improve my selling mindset			
7: Manage my sales team			

Delivery strategy Seven x7

Seven common challenges in delivery strategy

Delivery strategy checklist summary	Doing this!	Do more!	Start doing!
1: Considerations for a bigger business			
2: Work less and make more money			
3: Get my internal team to perform better			
4: Get my external team to perform better			
5: Find more of the right people			
6: Get better customers who pay more			
7: Stay in control whilst growing			

Financial strategy Seven x7

Seven common challenges in financial strategy

Finance strategy checklist summary	Doing this!	Do more!	Start doing!
1: Basic finances			
2: Overcoming numerophobia			
3: Generate more cash			
4: Use the numbers			
5: Plan for growth			
6: Spend my money wisely			
7: Fund a new venture			

Printed in Great Britain
by Amazon

54903143R00183